LOW
MAINTENANCE
GARDENING

FRANCES LINCOLN LIMITED
PUBLISHERS

LOW MAINTENANCE GARDENING

ANDI CLEVELY

PHOTOGRAPHS BY
STEVEN WOOSTER

Frances Lincoln Ltd
4 Torriano Mews
Torriano Avenue
London NW5 2RZ
www.franceslincoln.com

Reducing demands on your time
and energy need not mean an
uninteresting garden: options include
neat, easily tended raised beds
(page 1), vegetables and herbs
organized like an ornamental border
(page 2), and even the relaxed
profusion of eco-chic (right).

CONTENTS

INTRODUCTION

Low-maintenance gardening often seems to be an idea without a home. Reactionary gardeners treat the concept with disdain, as if it is slightly shameful – perhaps showing people how to avoid gardening – or betrays a long tradition of hard work and conscientious care. Environmentally aware gardeners commend any method that results in less interference and a reduced impact on our surroundings but condemn time-saving devices such as machinery, hard landscaping or hybrid plants. Kinder souls may simply express regret that making economies and taking short cuts somehow bypass the deeper joys of burying oneself in the garden.

Gardens are for people as well as plants: living rooms where you can work and tend flowers, or, if you prefer, relax (page 6) or entertain (left) in a beautiful but undemanding setting.

There are some who would like to toil outdoors from dawn to dusk but cannot, and many more who would rather not. This book and the low-management approach it describes are for those conditional gardeners: people who might be enthusiastic but are constrained by lack of opportunity or ability, and those who, for various reasons, are reluctant to devote the time and effort required by traditional gardening routines, but still want some kind of outdoor display or a pleasant setting for other open-air activities.

Being unwilling or unable to undertake some of the tasks recommended by most experts is no reason to give up gardening altogether. A common but unwise response is to hard-surface as much ground as possible, which might reduce the commitment required but often means that the exterior of the property looks sterile. Large areas of concrete or tarmac can also create serious drainage problems with sudden volumes of rainwater, as well as handing on a difficult legacy to a future owner who might want a garden. In a world where topsoil – one of its most precious resources – is vanishing twenty times faster than it is being made, conservation is preferable to camouflage.

The solution instead is to completely re-examine garden design and practice with the aim of gradually reducing the amount of work and attention required. The ideal of low maintenance is not incompatible with having a garden of beauty and bounty, and in many respects can be beneficial to plants and their surroundings. And it is an approach that successfully disposes of the old, rather despairing assertion that 'a gardener's work is never done'.

Traditional gardening

Although immensely satisfying for any who might survive the training, choosing a career as a professional gardener was never an easy option. An apprentice usually started with months of tedious but essential chores, such as scrubbing clay pots, mixing seed compost, washing down greenhouses or digging vast areas of bare ground.

Only when he (generations of working gardeners were almost exclusively male) had proved himself to be tractable, untiring and conscientious would he be allowed to move on to the most mundane of care routines involving plants. There could be an unending list of these, from staking dahlias, disbudding chrysanthemums and dead-heading rhododendrons to opening or closing rows of cold frames at dawn and dusk, hoeing endless rows of vegetables and hand-weeding asparagus beds. After a few years of increasing experience and confidence, the apprentice gardener might graduate to become a foreman or single-handed gardener somewhere, and ultimately perhaps a head gardener responsible for maintaining every aspect of daily life in a staffed garden. Visitors to stately homes today can appreciate that his brief might include looking after fine extensive lawns, water gardens, woodland and shrubberies, as well as maintaining a well-stocked kitchen garden, display houses and vineries, and even providing an unbroken display of cut flowers within the main house.

The demands on his varied skills were often exacting. On one famous estate the owner was renowned for lying down at the end of box hedges to check that they were trimmed with mathematical precision. At another a fresh orchid was required every morning in the master bedroom and daily vegetables at the kitchen door. The gardener was expected to grow everything and to grow it to the highest standard.

If he was articulate, he might eventually sit down to write a gardening manual filled with professional tips and inside knowledge, with an unfailing emphasis on what is now called 'best practice'. This almost invariably could be translated to mean intensive maintenance and full-time devotion.

The accumulated wisdom of such master craftsmen is still the basis of many gardening books and magazine articles today, passed on largely unquestioned and now enshrined as a kind of orthodoxy that many of us still accept. Departing from this established wisdom is almost heresy, always accompanied, it is implied, by the risk of courting disaster: gardening should be done properly or not at all, according to the traditional school.

A lesson from nature

In the past this counsel of perfection has daunted and sometimes deterred a lot of amateur gardeners, but happily attitudes have changed radically in recent decades, for a number of sound reasons.

An enlightened appreciation of our natural surroundings, and even alarm at the threats to its welfare, gradually replaced an ingrained fear that relaxing vigilance for a moment would inevitably invite weeds and

The apparent anarchy of a wildflower patch, here embellished with a little unobtrusive whimsy, is a simple low-maintenance solution that leaves nature to do most of the work.

wilderness back into the garden. Rediscovering the old cottage garden ideal made popular a more homely style, slightly rough at the edges, while wildflower gardening strove to rescue native plants and creatures from their decline in the open countryside and made many of us reconsider what was or was not acceptable in our gardens.

Popular science has helped us appreciate that some hallowed gardening routines are unnecessary and may be self-defeating. Tests have shown, for example, that digging does not always achieve the benefits claimed for it, and in many respects can be detrimental to the soil's structure and its teeming population of vital resident organisms. Keeping the soil surface bare and weed free is pointless, except to maintain appearance, because nature abhors a vacuum and empty ground invites more weeds. Excessive watering is harmful, whereas a more carefully targeted and rationed approach delivers water exactly where it is needed, at the same time avoiding waste.

Technology has come to the rescue of the hard-pressed gardener with various devices to automate watering and ventilation, while intelligent plant breeding has introduced varieties and cultivars that resist troublesome pests and diseases or thrive with less pruning or protection. Combine these with an awareness that nature generally looks after herself quite successfully without much encouragement or interference on our part, and all the elements are there for a fresh and more sustainable approach to gardening that can ensure it is a pleasure rather than a chore.

Asking the right questions

'Low maintenance' does not mean 'no maintenance'. The saying that anything worthwhile always involves effort is probably true, but the amount required in the garden can be reduced dramatically by co-operating with natural processes rather than dominating them. Finding an easier method depends on asking the right questions about your aims and ambitions, and evaluating the various assets in your garden. There are many reasons why you might need or prefer an easy-care garden, and understanding these can help you decide how to create your ideal kind of garden. Establishing this also depends on the nature of the site: if you are starting from scratch, it will be a simple matter of including those features you are prepared to accept, but an existing garden may need radical redesigning to reduce or eliminate unwelcome or unsuitable aspects.

Being selective is a cornerstone of any low-maintenance strategy. Trying to sustain the full range of traditional tasks with less input of time and effort is likely to end in frustration and a garden that looks shabby and neglected. By adopting instead a lighter, more streamlined workload, shedding those features and routines you dislike or that experience shows are in fact a waste of time, you can have an attractive, varied and flourishing garden with a fraction of the effort traditionally required.

Develop a strategy

The best way to reduce your commitment in the garden is to sit down and make a thorough reappraisal of the work involved.

- First assess honestly your ambitions, assumptions and attitudes about gardening.
- Take a fresh look at the garden itself, balancing any drawbacks against its assets.
- Reconsider its design and identify areas where you can simplify maintenance.
- Study your soil, which may be a major cause of unnecessary struggle.
- Make a wish list of plants, features and activities you cannot do without.
- Plan a programme of changes and a realistic timescale for achieving them.
- Decide where to install at least one seat where you can enjoy the time you have saved.

1

REALISM in the GARDEN

Gardening should alleviate stress, not produce it. Many of us have preconceived ideas about what is essential to ensure colour, variety and interest, and make inappropriate choices prompted by fashion, the gardening media or simply impulse buying. Even though most of a garden's components are taken from nature, the result is a completely unnatural arrangement of plants accustomed to a variety of different habitats and climates, all gathered together in conditions that may be alien, and even hostile, and looking after them can absorb a lot of time and devotion. Reappraising the reality on the ground with an open, honest mind can help achieve the dream of an appealing garden that almost looks after itself.

SOME BASIC PRINCIPLES

We all tend to do a multitude of jobs in the garden
dutifully without questioning their necessity or whether
they are worthwhile, particularly if we enjoy working
outdoors anyway or inherit plants and features that need
intensive care. Mowing once or twice a week from early
spring to late autumn, trimming hedges several times a
year, weeding large beds and training vigorous climbers,
digging heavy soil each autumn or pulling up weeds and
invasive ground cover, sowing under cover, transplanting,
staking, dead-heading: some or all of these chores are
often part of a typical gardening routine.

Concrete, machinery, pesticides and herbicides have
all been recommended at one time or another as
essential aids, but they are simply ways of coping with
the symptoms rather than removing the causes of a
demanding workload. They can indeed all save
considerable time and effort, but each has serious
intrinsic drawbacks. Concreting over ground causes
problems with water management, for example (see page
42); machinery like hedge trimmers, leaf blowers and
powered mowers produce noise and atmospheric
pollution; chemical sprays are environmentally unfriendly
and, like garden machinery, depend ultimately on a finite
energy supply for their manufacture and power.

Rather than try to perpetuate an onerous and
unwelcome schedule by one means or another, it might

Just a few choice easy-care plants can be enough to create a sympathetic garden setting, in containers on a decked roof (page 12) or planted in raised beds or through a gravel-topped membrane in an inviting nook (left).

be more sensible to make radical changes in the garden that reduce the burden, leaving only those features which are indispensable or easy to care for. Deciding what to keep or abandon starts with a frank self-appraisal.

DECIDING PRIORITIES

There are many reasons why looking after your garden might seem an overwhelming task. The overall design could be too complex and fussy, requiring more care and attention than you have the time or inclination to supply. Although once a delight, it might have outlived its value as a source of pleasure and beauty and, if you don't have your former stamina, ability or interest any more, become a burden. If so, it will need steering into new ways that suit your present lifestyle. Gardeners can evolve and change as fundamentally as their gardens.

Identify the things you enjoy most in the garden. You might be enthusiastic about your fine lawn, gaudy summer bedding, training and sculpting topiary or

A simple and effective way to reduce a familiar chore: while otherwise undemanding, this water garden (below right) depends on regular mowing to maintain its formal setting, whereas a garden meadow (top right) needs cutting only once or twice a year. A few passes of the mower take care of the grass path.

Contrasting schemes

An intensive garden might contain a lavish range of flowering plants, many of them from warmer regions; beds and borders planned according to colour or texture; a lawn that must look good while also supplying a playground for children; fast-growing hedges and shrubs for quick results; ground that is dug or hoed to look cared for; and seasonal surges of pests and diseases that constantly demand vigilance and some kind of intervention.

A low-maintenance garden could include fewer flower types, mainly perennials and in larger groups, chosen to suit the soil and setting; plants organized in compatible layers or tiers to make the most of limited resources; a lawn managed for low upkeep, with naturalized plantings, rough areas and site-specific grasses; slow-growing and 'self-cleaning' shrubs and informal or wildlife hedges; soil left undisturbed beneath mulches and ground-cover plants; and a stable balanced level of pests and their natural predators.

Framing a patio with generous raised beds brings life into an otherwise barren corner and allows you to tend and appreciate quite substantial plants at a comfortable height.

growing exhibition sweet peas, and be quite happy to give these all the attention they demand. If so, re-plan the garden around these activities, and reduce or simplify everything else that competes for your time. If all you want is a sophisticated setting for entertaining and relaxing, choose a few appropriate easy-care features and exclude everything else. Remember that you always have the option of deciding how much or little happens on your own patch.

Don't feel excluded by physical disability if gardening is your passion: impossible features can be eliminated, and others simplified or adapted to meet your needs. Raised beds can bring the ground up to a comfortable height if you find bending difficult, for example, possibly with wide intervening passageways for wheelchair access. A range of techniques are taught to blind gardeners, based on using simple square or rectangular low-maintenance beds of fixed size and managed from adjacent paths.

TOO MUCH GARDEN?

The size of the garden may be the problem, rather than its contents or design. Lack of space is the commonest complaint as modern gardens shrink ever further, but sometimes there is too much ground to look after with the available resources. There are a number of ways to reduce its size or maintenance, however, leaving a more realistic area to tend comfortably.

- Divide the garden into beds, improve and simplify one at a time, and simply cut down everything else occasionally until you are ready to proceed.
- Clean and improve small patches where you can plant easy-care shrubs (see pages 62–3), strimming or mowing the spaces between until the plants meet.
- Cut down growth and cover large areas with geotextile sheet topped with a mulch to control weeds, and plant choice plants through this.
- Cut down growth, mow one or two paths for access and encourage the rest to develop into a wildflower garden, easily tended just once or twice annually.
- Plant an orchard of favourite apple varieties on dwarfing rootstocks and keep the space in between strimmed or grazed with ducks.
- Develop a forest garden community of perennials (see page 25) that are attractive, productive and virtually self-reliant.
- Share the garden or rent part to a neighbour with no garden or who wants to grow vegetables.
- Above all, don't assume that pushing it out of sight under paving is the best solution.

Re-creating the typical community of shade-tolerant plants found on a natural woodland floor is much easier than trying to establish a conventional flower border in the dry shade of large trees.

ASSESSING THE GARDEN

Take a long careful look at your garden, not just from the most obvious viewpoint such as the backdoor but also from upstairs windows, the far end looking back to the

Hard landscaping doesn't have to be sterile or environmentally unfriendly: here timber and stone are used sensitively to create an attractive, all-weather patio with a hint of Far-Eastern calm.

Some possible changes

List features in the garden and then consider reducing any that appear in the first column while favouring those in the second.

Reduce:	Increase:
Fussy, demanding and over-vigorous plants	Shrubs with low pruning needs
Tender bulbs and annual bedding schemes	Permanent or naturalized bulbs
Invasive and weedy spreaders	Non-invasive ground-cover plants
Plants unsuited to the soil or site	Site-specific plants
Fragile and disease-prone plants	Resistant and tolerant varieties
Large, vigorous or untidy trees	Compact, slow-growing trees
Allotment-scale vegetable crops	Favourite crops in beds or containers
Invasive herbs	Hardy non-running herbs
Fine lawns	Tough, slow-growing lawn grasses
Half-hardy annual bedding	Self-seeding annuals
Perennials needing support or division	Slow-growing, self-supporting perennials
Bare ground and routine digging	Permanent mulches
Small pots and hanging baskets	Large, self-watering containers
Formal and quick-growing hedges	Fences, walls, informal hedges
Large borders and island beds	Narrow or raised beds
Grass or gravel paths	Hard but porous surfaces

house and even from a seat in the middle as well. Consider every aspect, such as its size and shape, the boundaries and surroundings, and whether it is sunlit most of the day or buried in deep shade.

If it is new, small or perhaps a tiny urban courtyard, this appraisal may not take long. Reacquainting yourself with a familiar established garden, on the other hand, could be a challenge unless you try to view it dispassionately, as if you were someone else seeing it for the first time.

Weigh up every feature and its value to you. Write a list if you like, annotating each item on a scale of one to five according to its importance. Be honest with yourself: a long-cherished feature like an asparagus or rose bed or a constantly weed-ridden rockery might seem indispensable, but if its upkeep taxes your time or ability, it should be marked as doubtful, if not definitely disposable. This is a very personal exercise, because only you know in your heart how much you can manage to do and which aspects of the garden merit your care.

And don't feel guilty about simplifying a demanding workload: it need not indicate laziness or weakness. Like the fashionable de-cluttering of personal belongings, deciding you no longer really need something is liberating and takes a load off your mind.

If soaking up the sunshine is a high priority, adapt the garden with this in mind, perhaps repaving a courtyard to make a green and intimate heat-trap (opposite) or creating a sunlit island patio enclosed by the suggestion of a flowering screen (above).

A LOOK AT DESIGN

When examining the overall design of your garden, it is crucial to keep a sense of purpose. You might dream of colour, profusion and thrilling beauty all year round, but any plan needs to be achievable in the context of the site and your overriding aim of avoiding unnecessary work and upkeep. Try not to be influenced by 'experts' who insist certain features or activities are essential, and by TV programmes that cheat or produce startling but impractical makeovers. Resist the irresistible.

Concentrate instead on what a garden means to you personally. Is it somewhere to collect and tend plants in the context of your time and ability, or are plants incidental, even irrelevant? You don't have to grow plants at all if you are a reluctant gardener. Perhaps your main use of the garden will be to exercise, dine al fresco, escape and relax with a book or beer at the end of the

The right plant in the right place can be an ally in your low-maintenance quest. Here *Osmunda regalis* or royal fern is a bold self-sufficient match for the demanding combination of wet soil, high humidity and low light levels.

Building a community

To get maximum performance with the least effort, compose your garden around a collection of hardy perennials – woody or herbaceous plants which live for several years without needing replacement, and which flower annually once mature – and organize them in a style that imitates the layered structure of natural vegetation, with plants growing at all levels where they can intercept enough light and other vital resources. In larger gardens the top level could be formed from restrained trees (see page 61) that cast dappled shade over a shrub layer immediately below; this can be surrounded and underplanted with herbaceous perennial flowers and a bottom tier of ground-cover plants. In small gardens shrubs will compose the top tier. Plant the sunnier patches with bulbs and self-seeding annuals.

working day, or as somewhere for your children to play within sight. Identify your main interest and keep this in mind; all else is secondary.

If you enjoy gardening, think about the style you prefer, because this can affect the amount of work involved. A formal garden, with trimmed hedges, a neatly edged lawn and a pattern of annual flower beds needs much more upkeep than a cheerful medley of trouble-free shrubs, perennials, bulbs and ground cover. The cottage garden style looks carefree but, unless you choose appropriate and compatible plants, you might have a lot of regular dead-heading, cutting back and seasonal clearing to do. Some themed gardens can be demanding if they depend on exotic or subtropical plants that on your site need protection from wind or frost. If the style you finally choose requires regular maintenance, look for ways to streamline its care and balance these demands by reducing any necessary work elsewhere in the garden.

Your answers to these searching questions will help you decide what to keep or exclude. There may be no need for many radical changes all at once – the best gardens evolve gradually, as will your ideas, as alterations take effect. Just modifying some features, one at a time, can make a difference. On sloping ground, for example, turning a path into a series of gentle steps may not reduce effort but can make distant parts of the garden seem more comfortably accessible. Moving the compost bin close to the house eases work because decomposition reduces the volume of waste materials by about nine-tenths, so there is always less compost to carry uphill than there are raw ingredients to take down.

Remember to consider the future in your plan for an easy-care design. Children grow up and leave home; your career or tastes could change. Even the climate probably has profound surprises in store: although many aspects of global warming remain unpredictable, extreme weather events seem increasingly likely, which may mean long hot spells in summer and heavier rain at other times. Early adaptation to cope with possible water shortages, drought, high winds and extreme heat is advisable if these are likely to affect your choice of activities or plants in the garden.

Make sure the site can match your vision. Deciding to concentrate on Mediterranean herbs rather than bog plants on waterlogged clay, for example, or to collect frost-tender architectural palms and tree ferns on a patio exposed to cold winds, might increase your workload as you strive to satisfy their needs. Steep slopes, seaside gardens, stony ground and deep shade are examples of site characteristics that might mean you have to adapt or compromise your plans if you are to avoid constant unnecessary work. Above all, you need to explore and understand your type of soil, which is crucial to success in any garden.

GET TO KNOW YOUR SOIL

There are many possible options in your mission to create an easy-care garden, but you cannot choose your soil (unless you grow everything in containers of compost, of course).

The main ingredient of every type of soil is rock that has been weathered and broken down over unimaginably long periods of time into tiny fragments. This mineral component will vary from place to place, depending on the type of bedrock under your garden: it may be the fine porous grains of sandstone, the lumpy flints and calcium-rich chunks of limestone, or a mixture of microscopic clay particles and stones from shale and mudstones. Whichever it is – and very often it is a blend of several kinds – its character is basically unchanging and will determine the behaviour of your soil.

All soils can be improved, however, to encourage stronger plant growth and simplify their care. Acid soil, for example, can be made more alkaline by adding lime, although the effect lasts only a few years and the technique is best reserved for local patches in the vegetable garden while you grow acid-loving plants elsewhere. Shallow topsoil can be augmented with bought-in supplies, either spread over the whole area or confined to raised beds where the effective soil depth can be increased even more (see pages 46–7).

Even the most adaptable and versatile flowers grow best where the soil satisfies certain conditions: oxeye daisies (*Leucanthemum vulgare*), for example, are a common ingredient of wildflower seed mixtures, but they are happiest in moderately fertile, well-drained sites.

Simple soil tests

- Find out more about your soil by digging a hole about 45cm (18in) wide and deep to show a cross-section of the dark topsoil and paler subsoil. This will indicate how far down plants can root before meeting relatively infertile conditions. Pour in a couple of cans of water and watch how long this takes to drain: an hour or less indicates good drainage, but several hours, even a day or two, could mean that you need to improve drainage or concentrate on growing bog and moisture-loving plants (see page 50).
- Squeeze a handful of moist topsoil into a ball: sandy soil will promptly fall apart again and feel gritty, whereas clay feels sticky and can be shaped or moulded, even polished with your thumb.
- Buy an inexpensive chemical soil-test kit (more reliable than electronic devices), and check samples of earth taken from various parts of the garden. The colour of the resulting test solution will give you a measure of the soil's acidity or alkalinity, and also indicate how you might adjust it for certain plant types. Most gardens are about midway between the two extremes and therefore capable of supporting a wide range of plants; seriously acid or alkaline soils have their own natural and lovely floras and it is best to choose plants happy with these levels rather than contrive radical changes.

Where amending the soil is difficult or expensive, try matching plants to its existing condition. There are species for every site, and identifying and understanding your soil type can often simplify choosing what to grow. Seaside soils, for example, are inevitably exposed to regular deposits of salt, which is toxic to some plants, but happily there are many others that positively revel in salt-laden ground (see page 74).

ADDING HUMUS

The most certain way to improve all kinds of soil is to add regular amounts of organic matter such as compost, manure or leafmould. These decay into the spongy substance called humus, which gives topsoil its dark colour and brings the simple rock component to life by hosting all kinds of organisms, from earthworms to microscopic mini-beasts that make the soil a more congenial place for plants to grow.

A high humus content reduces soil maintenance considerably. It changes the rock fragments into workable crumbs, binding sandy soil so that it absorbs more moisture and doesn't rapidly lose nutrients and water, and encouraging the fine particles of clay to clump together in crumbs, creating larger pores that admit air and allow the ground to breathe as well as helping surplus rainwater to drain away more quickly. Humus can even trap and immobilize heavy metals like lead, so reducing the risks of

It is said there is a primula for every situation, however extreme. The various kinds of Candelabra primroses provide a colourful and long-lasting solution for permanently moist soils with plenty of humus.

growing plants in contaminated soil near roads and industry. Dig in lavish amounts of compost initially, even if you have to buy it in, and then keep humus levels high by recycling all your waste into compost for spreading as an annual mulch (see page 102).

THE NEXT STEP

Do devote enough time to all these preliminary matters, and never make any irreversible decisions until you feel confident about where to make changes and why. Understanding your reasons for wanting to streamline the upkeep of the garden, and identifying areas or features that can be retained, discarded or amended, are essential first stages towards organizing more time to enjoy relaxing in the garden and less for actually working in it.

Your survey or re-assessment of the site will have identified its assets and constraints – the sunny sheltered angle where you ought to place a comfortable seat or even a hammock instead of an over-sized and demanding shrub, for example, or the cold or shady spots, awkward slopes and windy corners that limit what you can do or plant without extra work or expense, now or later. All this information will be invaluable when you start choosing new plants or building structures.

Appreciating the type and condition of the soil and the simple but effective ways of improving it should be essential for all gardeners, especially since taking soil for granted, especially if it is in poor condition, and then expecting it to perform well is a common drain on time and effort. Improving the soil and then growing those plants that suit it can be a huge first step towards your goal of low-care gardening.

The next step is to focus more closely on those areas or activities you intend retaining, and to explore ways of keeping their maintenance simple and straightforward. Some of these methods might be new, others old but well tested. Scepticism is a valuable tool in the garden, and it is always worth questioning everything, asking yourself if something is what you really want or need, whether it is worthwhile and suits your lifestyle or if there is an easier or quicker way.

And remember that even the finest garden is only nature organized to suit a plan or dream. How much organizing you undertake or decline is a personal choice that need not be accompanied by feelings of inadequacy: nature is very self-sufficient, and has managed to survive a long time with or without our intervention, which should be reassuring.

Remember that the infinite variety of leaf shapes, sizes and colours can offer an enormous repertoire from which to choose undemanding candidates to furnish a cool secluded corner.

Buy superior tools

While assessing the garden and your involvement with it, check that the tools you use are not causing unnecessary difficulties. Cheap and badly made tools make hard work of the simplest task. Always choose the best you can afford, testing their weight and balance, and rejecting any that might prove awkward or uncomfortable in prolonged use. Search out models that suit your height and grip – with longer handles or left-handed blades, perhaps; if you have heavy ground, avoid lightweight versions that could bend or break. Stainless steel is expensive but easy to clean and a pleasure to use, even in sticky soil. Keep tools clean and sharp for effortless use: a little care and attention can benefit both you and your plants.

2

SETTING the STAGE

Garden designers always consider the wider picture first, and establish an appropriate stage and background with which people and plants are comfortable. Although replacing plants or changing the way they are managed is often enough to reduce your commitment of time and effort, sometimes a more fundamental overhaul is necessary, especially if the garden developed haphazardly or the original plan was unsuitable in the first place. You might need to redesign the whole of your garden or just modify part of the layout, but getting the structure and setting right for your plans and priorities is a sound way to start creating a more manageable garden.

THE GARDEN LANDSCAPE

Professional gardeners who live on site often find it difficult to take a detached look at the place where they spend all their daylight hours: when you live 'over the shop' you see everything in terms of work. The same problem can arise if you try to stand back and assess your own private garden as a whole: sometimes it is indeed hard to see the wood for the trees.

Assessing the garden and its setting as a landscape where you feel at ease can be an enlightening exercise, however. Often it reveals basic flaws in the design or local spots that have got out of hand, and it can suggest where simple improvements might be made.

Problems may lie beyond the garden. You may have an tree overhanging from next door that shades and dries out part of your garden, for example; dark surrounding walls that plunge the whole garden in gloom for part of the year; or exposure to strong winds that regularly play havoc with your efforts to relax in the sun or grow favourite plants (a particular feature of seaside gardens). There is often a direct remedy, such as removing an intrusive branch or shielding the garden with windbreak plants, but if the problem is permanent, explore alternative solutions like using mirrors and light paint on a dark wall, arranging screens and overhead plants for shelter, or sourcing and matching plants that suit the environment.

Fitting your garden scheme into the wider landscape can make for easier management: a relaxed semi-wild style suits country surroundings (page 32), for example, while a rooftop setting (left) requires robust species carefully selected for healthy growth in exposed containers.

But most causes of unnecessary work arise on the property itself. Overgrown conifers and hedges, old diseased trees, a large demanding lawn, over-ambitious or intricately shaped beds and borders, areas that need the most care lying farthest from the house or at the wrong end of a stiff climb, meandering or weed-prone paths that logically go nowhere, a dilapidated fence that looks depressing or dangerous. The possible flaws might seem endless, but once you recognise any that might affect your garden and the upkeep it needs, you are halfway to finding a solution.

EARTHWORKS

Spot changes may be sufficient, but if a major redesign is the only realistic option, plan the work carefully, ideally starting by annotating a scale drawing of the site before and after the proposed changes. A complete makeover is often deeply satisfying but can be time-consuming and involve a lot of effort, so make sure it is worthwhile and where possible divide the undertaking into easy stages.

Seeking help

At all stages of a major undertaking it is worth considering professional assistance, both to relieve the workload and to ensure that the project runs smoothly and efficiently. Garden designers are familiar with low-maintenance specifications and can offer detached and informed advice. Any major or elevated tree work should be given to a qualified and adequately insured tree surgeon. All permanent structures need some kind of foundation, which you might prefer to leave to an experienced builder. And moving large volumes of soil will be much easier if you hire suitable machinery, with or without an operator.

If you plan to do the work yourself, check you have considered all the necessary precautions. New structures or changes to existing ones may need planning permission from the relevant local authority, as will any alterations to water flowing across or off your land. Locate and avoid underground services such as gas, electricity and water supplies, and make sure they are still easily accessible after work is completed. Watch out for tree roots, avoid disturbing building or boundary foundations and keep damp-proof courses well above finished levels.

Good fences and sound walls control the spread of ground-cover plants as well as supplying privacy, security and a visually pleasing low-maintenance boundary for a garden.

THE GARDEN BOUNDARY

A garden is an enclosure that needs some kind of defining boundary for security and privacy. This is usually an existing fixture that you have inherited and may be a wall, fence, hedge or a combination of these.

Walls Although expensive to build from scratch, a well-made brick or stone wall is virtually maintenance free. Even if it is in poor condition, it may need little more than re-pointing to restore the mortar joints. Walls of buildings in a poor state of repair might need brushing down, re-pointing and then coating with render or long-life masonry paint to be trouble free indefinitely.

Fences Quicker and cheaper to erect than walls, a fence is not so durable (expect a lifetime of 20–25 years for a solid, well-built fence) and, depending on its construction, may need regular painting or treatment with preservative. Keep it easily accessible: train climbers on trellis that can be lowered out of the way at maintenance

time. Replace an ageing fence rather than constantly repairing it; support an unstable post with a long-lasting concrete godfather; and make sure new posts are fitted with metal ground spikes to eliminate any risk of rot.

Hedges These take up more space than a fence or wall (for a new hedge, allow a 1m(3ft)-wide strip of soil), and need more regular routine care. This can vary from every six weeks between spring and autumn for species like privet and *Lonicera nitida* to once annually for an informal hedge of fuchsias, lavender or rugosa roses. Formal hedges with strict geometrical profiles need more frequent attention than informal flowering hedges (but these spread more widely). Dense thorny species such as blackthorn, holly and pyracantha make impenetrable barriers to intruders, while offering decorative flowers and fruit in return for a single annual trim to shape.

Looking after hedges

An established and well-maintained hedge of an appropriate species can provide all the benefits of shelter, seclusion and seasonal change with the minimum of care. Make sure the finished height is comfortably within reach – 1.2–1.8m (4–6ft) is usual – and that you can reach the far side of the top.

Clip all hedges with a gentle taper inwards towards the top, which admits light to the whole of the sides and prevents thin patches that might need later repair. If

Easiest boundary plants

- Beech (*Fagus sylvatica*) – formal, deciduous; trim late summer
- Berberis – many informal kinds, evergreen or deciduous; trim after flowering
- Escallonia – evergreen, informal, good for seaside gardens; trim after flowering
- Field maple (*Acer campestre*) – informal, deciduous; trim in late autumn
- Firethorn (*Pyracantha rogersiana*) – informal, evergreen, good berries; trim midsummer
- Holly (*Ilex aquifolium*) – dense, evergreen, formal; trim late summer
- Hornbeam (*Carpinus betulus*) – fast-growing, formal and deciduous; trim late summer
- Laurel (*Prunus lusitanica*) – evergreen, formal, large; trim mid-spring
- Western red cedar (*Thuja plicata*) – dense evergreen, trim mid-spring
- Yew (*Taxus baccata*) – evergreen, formal, green or gold; trim late summer

possible, keep the base of hedges clear enough for you to spread a sheet of polythene to catch the trimmings. Use sharp shears or a powered hedge trimmer, and divide the task of clipping large hedges into manageable stages, treating the sides and top as separate jobs if time presses.

Renovate overgrown and neglected hedges by pruning them hard back, one face at a time, in winter (deciduous species) or mid- to late spring (evergreens). Shredding and spreading the prunings as a mulch under the hedge can save you having to water and weed the area.

When planting a new boundary hedge, erect a temporary fence or windbreak in exposed positions to protect it while it is getting established, and space plants about 45cm (18in) apart for rapid dense growth. Trim off about one-third of the top growth after planting and annually thereafter until it develops a firm, well-branched structure – this can save a lot of unnecessary training or repair of gaps and thin patches. Where possible, avoid fast-growing species such as leylandii or Lawson's cypress, privet and box for formal hedges, because they need frequent precise trimming every year.

HARD SURFACES

Appropriate decisions about the design, siting and construction of paths and paving can substantially reduce the amount of maintenance you need to carry out in your garden. Obvious reductions in routine care can be made by covering a larger area of ground with hard landscaping, but even re-aligning or overhauling an existing surface can make surprising economies if the placing or materials were wrong to start with. A seldom-used path may become weedy or slippery with algae unless cleaned regularly, for example, while gravel can eventually accumulate soil and leaf debris and become dirty or host weeds, especially if laid directly on the ground.

Before deciding to extend the proportion of hard surfacing, it is important to consider the overall effect you are trying to achieve. Covering as much bare soil as possible might be a tempting and apparently easy solution, but the finished space could look dull and uninviting, might affect drainage and microclimate (hard surfaces shed water, reflect light and store heat), and will almost certainly alter the visual impact and apparent size or shape of the garden -– not necessarily for the better.

A paved area is almost always formal in style; it is functional, whether for relaxing and entertaining or outdoor activities; and if it is to blend in well, it should match the character of the buildings and surrounding area, in wet weather or dry. There is no gain if the result jars visually and ends up no more than an empty floor space to sweep occasionally.

Steps on gradients (left) and sound, comfortable paths across level ground (right) make a garden more inviting to access and explore as well as easier to tend.

Paths and steps

Like larger paved areas, paths and steps have a practical purpose. A path provides access, needs to lead somewhere – a dustbin, washing line or simply the end of the garden, for example – and should follow a well-worn route: laying a meandering path for the sake of appearance makes unnecessary work if everyone then takes a direct short cut instead. It should be wide enough for easy access to avoid damage to adjacent plants and features, and be surfaced with a durable material laid on a solid foundation.

Steps are simply changes in level of a path, and similar considerations apply to them in terms of function, planning and construction. Consider building steps if you have a demanding slope anywhere in the garden, as they are easier to negotiate and maintain, and make other garden chores less onerous. If your main priority is to reduce physical effort, plan deeper treads and shallow risers for less exertion: a consistent rise of 8–15cm (3–6in) and a tread depth of about 45cm (18in) should ensure a leisurely ascent or descent.

Surfacing materials

Surfaces vary widely in style, visual appeal and ease of installation. Some are more trouble free than others, while a few (especially concrete and asphalt) have serious disadvantages, so it is worth exploring the various merits of the commonly available materials.

Bricks and setts Attractive and informal in appearance, these are small units with numerous joints that may require regular weeding. They must be laid evenly on a firm bed, and can be expensive if you pay for the work to be done. Make sure bricks are weatherproof to avoid constant crumbling after frost; engineering bricks resist slippery algae and make the best choice for damp and shady places. Stone setts are much harder and more durable.

Slabs and pavers These are available in a range of sizes and shapes that can quickly cover a large area, sometimes in decorative patterns. Natural stone is the most expensive, concrete (with various textured finishes) the least. They are all very durable if well laid on a solid, thoroughly tamped foundation, and can be maintained in good condition more easily than bricks, but large areas can look dull unless relieved by plants or panels and edgings of contrasting materials.

Perforated brick paving set in sand or soil allows rainwater to infiltrate the ground beneath and mellows as mosses colonize the joints and hollows. To restore a pristine appearance, clean with a hired pressure washer and then top up joints by brushing in a dressing of sharp sand.

Easy-care water management

As more garden space is covered by patios, drives and parking areas, urban drainage systems are increasingly overwhelmed by sudden huge volumes of storm water. This happens especially when concrete, asphalt and similar impervious materials are used. This problem could be aggravated by the predicted increase in extreme and prolonged rainfall resulting from global climate change. Permeable hard surfaces are now preferred, as these allow rainwater to infiltrate the soil naturally and thus reduce ill effects such as flooding and building subsidence. For long-term low maintenance in the wider environment, surface drives with perforated bricks or mesh, fill paving joints with sand rather than mortar, and slope impervious surfaces to gulleys that channel and capture rainfall for garden use.

Timber decking A lightweight and easily manipulated material, perfectly suited to uneven ground and changes of level if installed on a solid sub-frame of joists and bearers. In wet districts the surface is liable to become slippery and discoloured by algae, so scrubbing or pressure washing may be necessary, at least annually. Durable hardwoods and decay-resistant cedar can be maintenance free for years, but softwoods, even when pressure treated, should be painted with environmentally friendly preservative annually.

Loose materials There is a wide choice of inexpensive and easily laid natural and decorative materials, from mineral aggregates such as gravel and shingle to less durable bark chippings and even shredded car tyres. They should be confined within an edging to prevent their spreading sideways on to beds, and laid on a weed-suppressant membrane to control invasion from below. All are easy to maintain with an occasional levelling with a rake, but tend eventually to trap soil, leaves and air-borne weed seeds. It can be difficult to walk or arrange garden furniture on some loose aggregates.

GROWING PLANTS IN CONTAINERS

Removing a plant from its home in the ground and confining it instead to a container might imply more

Containers come in all shapes and sizes to match the vigour and style of the potted plants. Terracotta pans and half-pots are best for a table-top display of succulents and tiny carpeting species.

maintenance, rather than less. Certainly, once potted up it is dependent on you for watering, feeding and general welfare, which may involve winter insulation, re-potting in spring and possibly twice-daily watering in hot weather. Despite the dedicated care they need, however, plants in containers are popular, instantly transform their surroundings and, in the case of a balcony, rooftop or paved courtyard, may be the only practical growing space available.

Rather than disqualify them as impossibly high-maintenance, explore ways to reduce their management.

Where the structure can support the load, roof-top plantings do best in deep capacious tanks or troughs for unrestricted root growth, moisture retention and resistance to extreme heat and cold.

- Larger containers stay moist for much longer, so group several plants together as a composition in a tub, planter or half-barrel, either transplanted or plunged to the rims of their individual small pots; check first they all enjoy the same conditions.
- Use a soil-based compost, which is more stable than soil-less mixtures. Add water-absorbent polymer granules to increase the available reservoir at the roots.
- To reduce water loss, line the sides of wood and ceramic containers with sheet plastic, and mulch the surface with bark, pebbles or a decorative aggregate – slate, glass and recycled copper granules are all efficient and colourful.
- Choose plants from dry habitats to reduce watering (see box), or make a water garden in a leak-proof container for growing marginal and aquatic plants.
- Arrange containers in groups for easier watering, and avoid putting them in a hot or windy position where they might dry out quickly.

Raised beds

A raised bed is really an enormous container filled with soil or potting compost to a comfortable working height, with the top and sometimes sides planted up as an elevated garden.

Raised beds have several great merits. The large volume of soil stays moist for long periods; plants can root and develop freely with little attention; and any

Drought-tolerant plants

A host of plant genera, many from naturally dry regions, can make forgiving candidates for containers and could reduce demands for frequent watering. They include *Agapanthus* • *Agave* • *Brunnera* • *Cistus* • *Cordyline* • *Geranium* • *Hedera* • *Helianthemum* • *Helleborus* • *Iberis* • *Lamium* • *Nerine* • *Papaver* • *Pelargonium* • *Penstemon* • *Pulmonaria* • *Sedum* • *Sempervivum* • *Senecio* • *Silene* • *Symphytum* • *Thymus* • *Verbascum* • *Yucca*.
Always check whether your choice prefers full sun or dry shade.

Water features need not be elaborate to add their unique contribution of light and movement to a garden. Even a simple and easily maintained canal of still reflective water is immediately eye-catching and makes the perfect accessory for a formal setting.

maintenance such as weeding may be done in a very short time without undue bending or exertion. Their depth – usually about 75–90cm (30–36in) – supports vegetables, shrubs and even small trees as well as annual and perennial flowers, while all-round access might allow a comfortable working width of 1.2m (4ft) or more. And you can tailor the soil mix to suit plants that might not thrive in the type or depth of soil in your garden.

WATER GARDENS

Looking after a pond or water feature is no more onerous than tending a bed or border, and if designed with care it can be a very low-maintenance asset, especially where it replaces a demanding patch of plants. In return for the initial hard work of installation, you will gain a unique source of light, movement and irresistible charm that can attract and benefit wildlife that could help you control many plant pests and diseases. You may choose to have just a still clear pool, perhaps with a few partially

Select plants according to the style of water feature. Moisture-loving perennials like primulas and Welsh poppies suit a secluded informal pool (left), whereas these minimalist stone bubble fountains (below) team perfectly with an equally stylized phormium.

immersed rocks for thirsty birds, or you may prefer to plant it with some of the numerous water-loving species that require little attention, least of all regular watering.

Ponds

Choose a site that receives at least six hours' sunlight in summer, well away from overhanging trees to avoid the autumn chore of fishing out submerged leaves. Construct the pond with a pre-formed plastic shell or flexible heavy-duty butyl liner, bedded on a 5cm (2in) thick layer of builder's sand, and include one or two shelves on which to sink plants to their preferred depths. If possible, site the pond close to an outdoor tap for topping up water levels in summer. As a refinement arrange an overflow link to an adjacent bog garden lined with a buried butyl sheet punctured here and there for drainage.

Water features

At the flick of a switch small moving water features such as pebble pools, wall spouts and millstone fountains supply music, movement and vitality quite

disproportionate to their size. They are safe, simple to install and require only annual cleaning and a pump service, and they may be arranged near a sitting or dining area, perhaps at a raised level for closer appreciation. Site them with the same care as ponds, and employ a qualified electrician to fit any electrical supply, unless the feature is driven by solar power.

Water plants

To ensure that a pond or water feature is virtually self-regulating, plan a balanced community of plant species. This creates a natural ecosystem that supplies essential shade and consumes dissolved nutrients, so reducing the risk of a green algal soup in summer (treat any outbreaks by submersing small packs of barley straw). You will need to supply one or two floating plants like water lilies or water soldier to shade about half the surface; a number of marginals such as water irises and marsh marigolds around the edge for colour, shelter and wildlife cover; and several submerged oxygenators such as hornwort or pondweed to maintain good water quality and clarity. Tidying and thinning these every spring is the only essential routine maintenance.

A collection of water- and damp-loving plants (opposite and left) is one of the easiest to maintain and needs only the constant presence of water, perhaps topped up from a gutter or rainwater butt overflow, to support such impressive perennials as *Rodgersia pinnata* (left).

GARDENING UNDER GLASS

Growing under glass makes you responsible for climate control and the daily task of ensuring adequate light, ventilation and heating levels for plants, as well as supervising their watering and feeding routines. On the other hand, many gardeners enjoy spending time in a greenhouse, where plants – often unusual or tender kinds such as cacti or alpines – are kept at a comfortable working height and the weather outside becomes irrelevant. Only you can decide if the rewards outweigh the extra responsibilities.

You can reduce the responsibilities by investing in automation, which is expensive but effective.

- Automatic vent openers are almost essential for all greenhouse gardeners, not just those aspiring to minimal maintenance. Once adjusted to the desired setting, these will open and close windows as often as necessary to prevent the normal wild fluctuations in temperature on sunny or cloudy days.
- Various automatic and semi-automatic irrigation devices can eliminate daily watering. Sand benches and capillary matting maintain a permanently moist substrate from which pots absorb water as required, while trickle systems keep pots moist via adjustable tubes and nozzles. All kinds can draw water from a header tank, which needs refilling occasionally, or direct from a

The controlled environment of a glasshouse offers protection to plants, from frost-shy exotics to the first strawberries, the latter readily forced into early production in 13–15cm (5–6in) pots without extra heat.

Most gardeners enjoy pottering gently in the congenial surroundings of a lean-to greenhouse or conservatory, an economical asset where plants may be propagated inexpensively or stored in cold weather for summer display in outdoor patio containers.

mains supply fitted with a cut-off valve and timer.

- Automatic blinds respond to light levels to help maintain optimum temperatures indoors. Alternatively you can cover the roof with shade netting in mid-spring and remove it again in mid-autumn – a far less onerous method than obscuring the glass with shade paint.

3

The ORNAMENTAL GARDEN

Flowering plants have been around for much longer than the human race – certainly well before we began looking after them in our gardens – and over the course of millennia colonized almost every kind of soil and site, where they managed to achieve self-sufficiency. Much of the work we assume needs doing in the garden results from growing plants in the wrong place or forcing them to behave in unnatural ways, and we can often save a lot of time and effort if we study their requirements and make realistic choices. This change of emphasis is a practical first step towards an effectively self-regulating flower garden.

CHARACTER STUDY

Flower gardening is sometimes seen as an exercise in design and decoration, with plants being chosen and arranged like ornaments in a room. But plants are living organisms with individual, often very specific needs that must be satisfied if they are to thrive unattended. Disregarding this basic but often overlooked aspect of their nature can involve us in failure, disappointment and avoidable work, whereas seeing gardening as a partnership between plants and gardener can be a more relaxed and creative policy. Although assessing low-maintenance needs starts from the gardener's perspective, finding a solution often comes from understanding plant personalities.

Whatever its visual appeal to us in a catalogue or garden centre, any plant can fulfil its potential in a particular niche or habitat only where it finds resources to its liking: beware of impulse buying anything before you discover its pedigree or character! The kind of conditions every plant requires include:

- **light** – this controls growth because plants convert sunlight into energy, and the more they receive, the more vigorously they grow;
- **water** – every plant needs a certain amount of water to dissolve food in the soil and make it available to the roots, to circulate these nutrients within the top growth

The simplest and most effective displays often depend on little more than a packet or two of seeds broadcast direct (page 54), or a perennial planting composed mainly around a single keynote species or variety such as these weather-proof echinaceas (right).

and to supply enough pressure to keep its stems firm;

- **nutrients** – for healthy growth and development, a range of essential major and minor food materials must be accessible;
- **air** – plants use carbon dioxide to assist the process of turning sunshine into energy, and oxygen in the atmosphere and the soil to make this energy available to their tissues as well as fuelling transpiration (breathing through the leaves).

Most of these resources are finite, so plants compete for them with their neighbours. They also differ widely in the amounts they use, which is why some can cope with shade, drought or waterlogged ground better than others. Members of a natural plant community or a well-balanced garden scheme complement each other, sharing the limited resources by growing or flowering at different times of the year or by fitting into a favourite niche where others might not thrive. A compact leafy woodland plant enjoys the shade beneath a more light-demanding shrub, for example, while spring bulbs often bloom and seed

themselves before the foliage of deciduous trees and climbers appears and obscures the sun.

WHERE WE OFTEN GO WRONG

Sometimes the worst qualification any gardener can have is a passion for gardening, because then the constant compulsion to do things may lead us to tinker with plants when no interference is necessary. When a plant is happy, it grows well (weeds are a perfect example of this principle, their easy-going tolerance allowing them to flourish in most habitats); if it is part of a compatible community, competition will prevent it from getting out of hand to the point where it must be cut back; and if any of its resources runs low, growth will slow down or stop, which often stimulates flowering in place of more foliage. A plant in the right place rarely dies from a bad season, except in extreme weather events (when we genuinely need to intervene).

Unfortunately lavishing tender loving care on plants is often irresistible, even though they are naturally self-sustaining and self-regulating, and can result in enormous amounts of work that is unnecessary.

- There is no need to dig or fork the soil between flowering plants every year, burying compost or manure that will feed excessive, often soft and vulnerable

Choosing flowering plants

Before deciding to buy a new plant that appeals to you, find out all you can about its credentials and preferences, so that you can match it with a suitable home. In particular check:

- maximum height and spread, to avoid needless pruning;
- whether it can fit into the existing garden, perhaps as part of the canopy or an understorey;
- the kind of soil it likes – acid, alkaline or average, and moist or dry;
- its ideal aspect – how much sun or shade it likes, and possibly shelter from wind;
- if it is fully hardy in your locality, to avoid the need for winter protection;
- whether it is evergreen and leafy all year, or deciduous and bare or invisible in winter;
- when and for how long it flowers, to assess how it fits into the plant community;
- other assets such as decorative fruits, outstanding foliage or attractive stems;
- possible flaws: a need for support or training, perhaps, or predisposition to disease.

growth. Nor do beds and borders of perennials usually require regular dressings of fertilizer.

- Keeping the soil between flowers bare and hoed clean is futile: empty ground invites weeds as well as allowing water and nutrients to escape into the atmosphere, whereas in natural communities soil is insulated under ground-cover plants or a mulch of fallen leaves.
- Frequent and regular watering of established plants should be superfluous if they are planted in suitable positions; wilting foliage is often a temporary survival reaction to hot sun or drying winds rather than a symptom of imminent demise.
- Managing the garden as an extension of the home with everywhere neat, clean and tidy is inappropriate when nature hides order beneath a casual appearance and plant communities are always a little dishevelled at the edges.

If you can relax the way you rule the garden, allow plants a little more independence and let them do the hard work, you should find yourself investing less time and effort in its upkeep, with proportionately more opportunity to enjoy it or do something else altogether.

Birches are stunningly beautiful trees, happy in most gardens, where they may be grown solo, as multi-stemmed clusters or in orderly groves (above), as full-size trees or pruned, even coppiced, to control their size.

GARDEN TREES

Woody perennials like trees, shrubs and climbers compose the upper, permanent storeys of the garden community, and build a framework that adds height and substance all year round. Trees form the canopy at the top – larger plots might have space for several, small gardens just one or two – and can create valuable shade and shelter for plants growing beneath. They may be deciduous (losing their leaves every autumn) or evergreen

As part of a community or as a solitary, easily managed garden or container star, slow-growing *Cornus controversa* 'Variegata' never fails to please, with its orderly tiered structure, white flowers and sunnily variegated foliage.

Some easy-care trees

Abies koreana • *Acer davidii* • *Albizia julibrissin* 'Rosea' • *Amelanchier canadensis* and *A. lamarckii* • *Buddleja alternifolia* • *Cornus florida* • *Crataegus laevigata* 'Rosea Flore Plena' • *Eriobotrya japonica* • *Ginkgo biloba* 'Fastigiata' • *Gleditsia triacanthos* 'Sunburst' • *Lagerstroemia indica* • *Magnolia stellata* • *Malus* 'Red Sentinel' and *M.* 'Royalty' • *Pinus mugo* 'Compacta' • *Prunus subhirtella* 'Autumnalis' • *Sorbus hupehensis*.

(also shedding leaves, but sparsely throughout the year), and they have a range of sizes, shapes, vigour and decorative value.

Choose a new tree carefully, according to its purpose and the site available. An evergreen could screen out wind and shelter less robust plants, shade the ground enough to suppress other growth and make an active contribution to garden's appearance all year round. Deciduous species with colourful stems or an elegant branch structure can also have winter appeal, while their seasonal loss of foliage allows woodland and spring-flowering plants to thrive beneath, but clearing their dead leaves in autumn may be irksome (although a valuable source of humus – see page 102).

Trees can create other problems, especially when an unsuitable species has been planted or allowed to get out of hand. The best kinds for most gardens are locally hardy and unaffected by pests or diseases, grow slowly and look attractive for most of the year, require little or no pruning, do not throw up suckers or shed messy fruits, and combine amicably with neighbouring plants. This specification excludes many familiar trees: for example, many willows grow fast and can disturb drains or foundations; some limes attract aphids and drip honeydew everywhere; yew can bear extremely sticky berries; and common lilac, despite its glorious blooms, produces suckers, needs pruning to flower lavishly and looks uninspiring for the rest of the year.

Sometimes the remedy is obvious – removing one or two misplaced or overhanging branches from an overgrown tree might admit enough extra light, for example. Or you can consult a qualified tree surgeon if you have doubts about what to do. Unless it is dangerous, diseased or totally inappropriate, explore all the alternatives before having a tree felled and removed altogether. Options could include crown reduction (lowering and thinning the canopy), raising the crown (cleaning the trunk to admit light from the sides) or coppicing, a method of cutting tolerant species down to ground level to rejuvenate growth. With this last method several new shoots arise, which can be singled to create a new tree of more controlled size, or you could leave them to make a multi-stemmed group (birch is a perfect subject for this treatment).

Prostrate shrubs such as this *Cotoneaster horizontalis* make efficient ground cover, hugging the contours and eventually shading out competition, except for a few determined and compatible kinds like grasses and ferns.

FLOWERING SHRUBS

Although extraordinarily diverse in shape, appearance and behaviour, all shrubs are woody, multi-stemmed perennials that branch at ground level, a characteristic that distinguishes them from trees with their single stems. Shrubs can vary in size, from tiny prostrate alpine willows like *Salix reticulata*, ideal for troughs and window boxes, to tree-like acers and elders 6m (20ft) or more tall and wide. They may be evergreen or deciduous, many are noted for their beautiful flowers or fruits, and some have glorious autumn tints of red or gold.

Shrubs are important low-maintenance plants because a single specimen can often fill a large space with attractive colour and form in return for little routine attention. When planting several, make sure they produce a balanced and visually exciting group with a sequence of flowers, fruits and fragrance. Avoid species that are borderline hardy (hibiscus, for example), short-lived (cytisus) or naturally shapeless (tamarisk).

Explore different forms of a particular shrub to find the perfect candidate for your site. You might love the flowers and fragrance of mock orange (*Philadelphus*), for example, but common kinds can exceed 4m (13ft) in height and spread, and then require ruthless pruning, whereas cultivars like 'Belle Etoile', 'Lemoinei' and 'Manteau d'Hermine' are more compact and restrained. There is an almost infinite range of variants from which to choose the ideal new shrub. Here is a basic selection.

Large structural shrubs (more than about 1.8m/6ft) create a framework, focal point or shelter: buddleias, *Euonymus alatus*, mahonias (especially *M. japonica*), *Osmanthus delavayi*, rhododendrons, spotted laurel (*Aucuba japonica*), smoke bush (*Cotinus*), viburnums (especially *V. tinus* cultivars) and witch hazels (*Hamamelis*).

Medium shrubs (60cm/2ft–1.8m/6ft) provide the main 'bones' of a flower border and can fill in between or under larger shrubs: berberis, choisya, cotoneaster, escallonia, hydrangea, hebe, hypericum, pieris, *Rhododendron yakushimanum* cultivars, ribes, *Skimmia japonica*, spiraea and *Viburnum davidii*.

Dwarf shrubs (under 60cm/2ft), including many prostrate conifers, make good ground cover, helping to smother weeds and keep the soil evenly moist and shaded:

Roses

The assumption that all roses need a lot of care is a fallacy, and if you are seeking a low-maintenance garden there is no need to deprive yourself of their unique colours, forms and fragrance. Least demanding in terms of dead-heading, feeding and pruning are unsophisticated and unimproved kinds such as *Rosa rubrifolia* or *R. xanthina* 'Canary Bird'; shrub roses (which tend to be close to wild species) such as 'Penelope', the English Roses series or the numerous *R. rugosa* hybrids; and ground-cover varieties like 'Flower Carpet', 'Surrey' and related county names. All can be clipped to shape if necessary with secateurs, shears or a hedge trimmer in early spring. Wherever possible, choose varieties with good disease resistance.

Popular climbers such as Virginia creeper, Boston ivy and many vines offer a range of talents, including attractive flowers, fruit, foliage and (as above) startling autumn tints as nights cool and leaves prepare to fall.

Arctostaphylos 'Emerald Carpet', *Berberis empetrifolia* and *B. thunbergii*, *Cotoneaster horizontalis*, *Daphne laureola*, *Escallonia rubra*, *Euonymus radicans*, *Gaultheria procumbens*, heathers, *Hypericum calycinum*, hyssop, *Juniperus communis* 'Depressa Aurea' and *J. horizontalis* 'Glauca', *Potentilla fruticosa*, ruscus, vinca.

CLIMBERS

Climbing and rambling plants have solved the problem of finding enough light by hoisting themselves up from their shaded root zone (most are woodland species) and infiltrating other supporting plants until their flowers find the sun. Gardeners have tended to take them away from their natural habitats and display them instead on walls, fences and free-standing structures like arches, pergolas and obelisks, where full exposure to light often controls

their vigour, but growing them in isolation usually means having to provide them with artificial support (see box on page 66).

Climbers may be perennial or annual, evergreen or deciduous, and you can have them in flower at almost any time of the year, depending on species and variety, especially if you include 'wall shrubs' in your selection. These are not true climbers, but produce tall flexible stems that usually look most effective when trained on supports; several kinds, such as winter sweet

Least demanding of all climbers for house walls are the self-supporting kinds like *Hydrangea anomala* subsp. *petiolaris* (above), which use aerial roots to gain height. Make sure walls and mortar joints are sound before planting.

(*Chimonanthus*), winter jasmine, pyracantha and chaenomeles supply welcome colour during the darker months.

With their scandent habit all these plants add height to the garden display by using vertical surfaces like fences and house walls; thus they extend the growing space

How climbers climb

There are several adaptations climbing plants have evolved in their scramble for light, and recognizing these can help you supply the appropriate kind of support.

Aerial roots Ivy, climbing hydrangea and *Campsis radicans* develop short clinging roots wherever their stems touch a vertical surface. At first they may need tying on canes until self-sufficient; make sure wall surfaces are sound.

Tendrils A common kind of holdfast: plants like sweet peas, clematis and passionflowers have modified stems, leaves or leaf stalks that coil round slender supports; Virginia creeper's tendrils end in suckers that stick to smooth surfaces.

Twining stems The shoot tips of runner beans or hops rotate until they find a slim support round which to wind: bamboo canes, poles, wires and even string can be used, depending on the type of plant.

Spines Plants such as roses and brambles have downturned thorns or prickles that hook on to any handy support, making them self-reliant in trees; elsewhere provide trellis or wires and tie in stems as they grow.

Perennial climbers such as clematis or rambler roses and annual nasturtiums, cobaea or thunbergia can be grown without support and left to sprawl as a colourful ground-cover carpet, particularly down steep banks, or to trail over a wall or balcony in floral swags.

without occupying much ground. Nor do they necessarily involve the gardener in a lot of extra work. Providing a climber with a position where it can achieve its full height and spread reduces pruning to a minimum, and any that may be required is usually pleasant work, at a comfortable height, for a sunny afternoon.

It is particularly important when choosing climbers to find out the ultimate size and preferred site. A climbing rose like 'Danse du Feu', for example, can just reach the top of a 2.4m (8ft) pillar, whereas 'Rambling Rector' will cheerfully romp 7.5m (25ft) or more into a large tree or over a north-facing house wall. Russian vine (*Fallopia baldschuanica*) is often planted to cover an eyesore, but it will twine up to 15m (50ft) in any direction in a sunny moist position and frequently causes more problems than it solves.

The ground next to trees and walls can be much drier than the open garden, so when planting climbers here add plenty of humus to create the moist root run they enjoy, and mulch all round afterwards; in a drought make these sites a high priority in your watering strategy (see pages 101–3). And remember that a mature canopy of climber foliage can be very heavy when wet, especially in a wind-prone position, so providing robust support can be a vital way to save work in the long run.

A vast selection of hostas is available for easy ground cover in sun or shade; dual purpose perennials with attractive foliage and flowers, many can reach 90cm (3ft) or more in height and spread. Their only enemies are slugs and high winds.

HERBACEOUS FLOWERS

Non-woody annuals, biennials and perennials form the lowest tier of natural vegetation. They vary from grasses (page 70), ground-covering creepers (page 73) and bulbs (page 75), to fast-growing ephemeral annuals (page 69) and a host of varied herbaceous perennials. They all have a place in the low-maintenance garden as well as a role to fill in a well-balanced and self-regulating plant society.

Perennials

Although almost any kind of plant, from oak tree to lawn grass, may strictly be a perennial (living indefinitely and for at least two years), gardeners use the term to describe hardy border flowers, the mainstay of most gardens.

They were traditionally grown in beds and borders by themselves, where they were organized according to height, flowering time or sometimes a colour theme, and then carefully thinned, staked and dead-headed, and periodically divided and replanted in freshly prepared soil.

For beauty without bulk in narrow borders against walls, choose airy heat-loving and drought-tolerant perennials that produce tall slender flowers from low compact clumps of foliage, such as these agapanthus, acanthus and *Verbena bonariensis*.

In this way they have unfairly acquired a reputation for demanding constant attention.

For a more relaxed approach that minimizes their essential care, balance hardy perennials with shrubs, grasses, bulbs and ground-cover plants in the kind of cohesive and self-sustaining plant community found in wild examples of your garden habitat. Whether that habitat is sunny or shaded, moist or dry, and on acid or alkaline soil, there are hardy, self-supporting and sociable perennials that can persist there happily rather than precariously, as many do when allied to unnatural companions and untenable positions.

Even when edited down to constitutionally suitable kinds, the range of possible species and varieties is huge and constantly growing. It is often more useful to know what to avoid (the need for staking, frequent division, disease control or protection from frost, for example), and then make a shortlist of a few favourites – perhaps eryngiums, salvias, stachys and verbascum in hot dry positions; astilbes, hostas, ligularia and pulmonaria for damp ground; or epimediums, geraniums, mertensia and

More easy perennials

Try some of these resilient and dependable stalwarts of mixed plantings:
Acanthus mollis and *A. spinosus* • achillea • *Ajuga reptans* • *Alchemilla mollis* • *Anemone hupehensis* • *Anthemis tinctoria* • aquilegia • arum • aruncus • astrantia • bergenia • *Crambe maritima* • *Dicentra spectabilis* • *Echinacea purpurea* • erigeron • *Euphorbia characias* • *Helleborus argutifolius* • hemerocallis • heuchera • *Iris sibirica* • knautia • kniphofia • liriope • *Lychnis coronaria* • nepeta • *Oenothera* 'Fireworks' • *Penstemon heterophyllus* • *Phlomis russeliana* • pulmonaria • *Rudbeckia fulgida* • *Sedum spectabile* • *Solidago* 'Golden Wings' • *Tradescantia* Andersoniana Group • *Veronica spicata*.

The evening primrose (*Oenothera*) genus is a suitable candidate for a warm position on very light, well-drained soil – and the sunshine and sand of a seaside garden make the ideal habitat for these yellow (very occasionally pink) perennials, which flower from midsummer onwards.

sanguinaria in deep shade. Plant lavishly and closely, mulch generously, and then leave them alone to merge and mingle. In autumn cut down all exhausted top growth, if you are tidy-minded, or leave it over winter to shelter foraging birds and clear away in spring.

Annuals

Do not dismiss annuals as transitory high-maintenance plants just because they need sowing or planting and clearing every year. They have an important role to play in

The flowers and seed heads of most grass species and cultivars have a unique mercurial beauty from summer well into winter, changing their appearance depending on whether they are sunlit, misted with dew or embroidered with frost.

natural plant communities, where they quickly fill bare spaces between perennials and cover the ground while their slower-growing neighbours are still developing, and they can supply a vivid and varying display, sometimes of instant colour, that is unrivalled by other plant types. Annual bedding plants (many of which are strictly hardy or tender perennials) are justly popular for spring and summer schemes in beds and containers.

You can reduce the amount of care annuals need by not growing them indoors from seed or cuttings (for alternative methods, see page 100), by choosing kinds that match the soil, aspect and exposure, and by concentrating on long-flowering and weather-resistant varieties that do not require dead-heading (these are often described as 'self-cleaning'). Many hardy annuals can be sown where they are to flower – in autumn for early blooms or mid-spring for later colour – and left unthinned. Choose a few of your favourites and allow

them to self-seed in their own niches to save future sowing: sweet Alison (*Lobularia*), calendula, coreopsis, candytuft (*Iberis*), nasturtiums, nigella and limnanthes will often reincarnate themselves year after year.

Grasses

Whereas lawn species need constant attention (see page 77), ornamental grasses are some of the easiest plants to care for, largely because they can be allowed to follow their natural life cycles, fattening and flowering without our restraint. Use them to replace part of a lawn, to provide contrasting form and foliage among broad-leaved plants, or even to compose an exclusive bed of their own. They range from neat, compact kinds such as bun-like *Festuca* 'Silver Sea' to aristocratic miscanthus, cortaderia and arundo varieties, any one of which could make a magnificent sculptural feature. Most form distinct clumps or tussocks (avoid those that run and invade other

Just some of the multi-faceted flower arrangements sported by
the huge range of desirable grasses, including the upright,
tightly packed plumes of robust *Cortaderia selloana* 'Pumila',
one of the tidier, more compact forms of this robust genus.

Provided it expands steadily and efficiently, a spreading species may be used to cover ground, from showy *Phlomis russeliana* (opposite) to the tiniest raoulias, soleirolias, creeping thymes or prostrate mint for filling cracks, crevices and larger patches of vacant ground (left).

plants), so grow them through a mulched membrane (see page 76) or team with broad-leaved ground cover. Grasses need no support, look appealing right through to seed head stage and need cutting down (perennials) or clearing (annuals) only once a year in spring.

Ground-cover plants

Planting for ground cover has a poor reputation with some gardeners, mainly because of a few rampant perennials notorious for trespassing far and wide through and over their neighbours. Exuberant colonists like dwarf periwinkle (*Vinca minor*) and yellow archangel (*Lamium galeobdolon*) are indeed to be avoided in confined spaces, but it is worth exploring the host of other spreading but well-behaved herbaceous plants and shrubs that can save labour in the garden by suppressing weeds, shielding soil surfaces and stabilizing ground with their mats of roots and stems.

Try to remove all weeds, including fragments of perennial roots, before planting, and then choose types according to the site:

Growing through a membrane

You can easily protect soil, prevent evaporation and suppress weeds in small areas by spreading a black plastic or geotextile membrane over clean cultivated ground. Use this to underlie gravel on paths or drives, and for a variety of planting schemes: simply cut a small cross in the fabric wherever you want to plant, tuck the flaps back round the plant afterwards and re-level the gravel or other covering.

- A rock garden can be one of the most demanding features to look after. Try the alternative of growing alpines and rockery plants like gentians, dianthus and saxifrages through a membrane, and then disguise the sheet with small rocks and stone fragments such as coloured slate to resemble a natural scree.

- In hot dry districts whole beds can be made with gravel over a membrane, planted with drought-tolerant perennials such as verbascum, kniphofia, lavender and heleniums, or annuals like poppies and marigolds. Similar plantings can embellish drives and other larger gravelled areas.

- Although delightful in other respects, a seaside garden is exposed to frequent drying winds that are also salt-laden when blowing inland, and these make huge demands on plants. Grow tolerant kinds like thrift, senecios, catananche and osteospermums through a membrane topped with sand and shingle, and shelter them with a robust hedge of olearia, euonymus or sea buckthorn (*Hippophae*).

- varieties of moss, raoulia and soleirolia to creep along soil- or sand-filled cracks and joints in paving;
- wild violets or *Erigeron karvinskianus* to edge and soften steps, low walls and the sides of paths;
- climbers like ivy (for shade), everlasting sweet pea (on chalk), clematis (moist soils) and rambler roses (full sun) to cover steep banks;
- erica, calluna and daboecia cultivars to blend together in a whole tapestry bed to themselves;
- various cranesbills (geranium), symphytum and violets for carpets under trees and shrubs;
- prostrate shrubs like *Cotoneaster procumbens* and *Juniperus horizontalis* for dense, ground-hugging evergreen foliage;
- tiarella, pachyfragma or globularia for tenacious roots to bind loose or disturbed soil.

Bulbs

True bulbs and their allies (corms and tubers) are ideal low-maintenance flowers that not only require minimal care but positively resent disturbance. Each is a neat package of dormant flower bud, leaves and stored food, and simply needs burial at the right depth in a suitable position, where it can settle down to flowering every year and multiply by seed or offsets into mature clumps. By choosing appropriate kinds you can have a sequence of blooms, from winter aconites and the earliest snowdrops at the turn of the year until the last displays of

Bluebells (above), although native woodlanders, will enhance almost any situation where they get enough spring sunshine to complete their flowering and growth cycles before midsummer. Easily grown lady's mantle (opposite) is equally content in woodland or growing through gravel-topped membranes.

There are hardy cyclamen species for every season of the year, flowering in winter, spring, summer or, as here, autumn, when *Cyclamen hederifolium* bears its dainty pink blooms and prettily marbled, ivy-shaped leaves. Just supply plenty of humus such as leaf litter, and avoid full sun and waterlogged soils to ensure continual success.

Reliable bulbs

There is almost a surfeit of choice of bulbs for temperate gardens. The hardiest and most dependable for permanent planting include
winter aconites (*Eranthus hyemalis*) • alliums (flowering onions) • anemone species such as *A. blanda* • bluebells (*Hyacinthoides*) • camassia • colchicums • spring and autumn crocuses • cyclamen (especially *C. coum* and *C. hederifolium*) • daffodils • dodecatheon • erythroniums • fritillaries • grape hyacinths (*Muscari*) • *Iris reticulata* • leucojums • lilies • ornithogalum • puschkinia • snowdrops • squills (*Scilla*) • and species tulips such as *T. springeri* and *T. sylvestris*.

colchicums, autumn crocuses and sternbergia. If rhizomatous plants are included in this group, you could add schizostylis to prolong flowering through the winter.

For easy maintenance, make sure the types you choose are hardy in your locality or have the protection of a warm wall if they are borderline (nerines, for example), and that they will survive a typical winter left in the ground – many summer-flowering bulbs like gladioli, ixias and sparaxis must be treated as annual bedding and lifted and dried off in autumn and replanted every spring. Plant them in suitable sites: spring-flowering bulbs tend to be woodland species and appreciate dappled sunlight, whereas summer and autumn kinds prefer full sun. Most like good drainage, although camassias, many anemones and *Narcissus bulbocodium* thrive in very moist soil.

Plant all bulbs at their favourite depth (the rule of thumb is to cover them with a depth of soil two to three times their own measurement from tip to base), in autumn for spring-flowering kinds and spring for all others. To ensure good drainage, in wetter ground plant sensitive kinds like alliums and lilies on their sides, instead of upright, or bed them on a handful of grit or sharp sand. Arrange bulbs in natural groups rather than singly at wide spacings, especially if you are naturalizing them in grass (see page 78). Allow their foliage to wither to recharge the bulbs. If the sight of their fading leaves offends, plant them next to spreading perennials or over-sow with an annual flower like love-in-a-mist (*Nigella*) for disguise.

LAWNS

Conventional advice suggests giving up a lawn if you want a care-free garden. This traditional centrepiece of many gardens can absorb a disproportionate amount of attention if maintained to a high standard – weeding, spiking, scarifying, edging, feeding twice annually and mowing every week from spring to autumn (possibly all year if the climate continues to warm up) – and this an obvious area where economies might be made.

Many people are strongly attached to their lawns, however. An expanse of turf is a visual oasis and a popular living space for outdoor activities and, understandably, you may be reluctant to abandon this key feature altogether. The practical solution is to modify its maintenance.

A change of policy

There are various grades of lawn grass, from robust play mixtures based on rye grass that shrug off shade, drought and hard wear, to the finest (in every sense) bents and fescues that create a superior bowling green and all the responsibility that goes with it. If you are planning a new lawn, choose turf (sowing grass is more complicated) from the utilitarian end of the range and have it laid for you. Reappraise an existing lawn to see if you can reduce its size, perhaps by building a patio or paved area for relaxation. Streamline its shape by abandoning island beds and fussy detail, rounding off square corners and adapting the width of grass paths to match one or more full passes of your mower.

Then relax the care regime.

- The more grass is mown, the faster it grows, so extending intervals between cuts and raising the finished height to about 4cm (1 1/2in) can dramatically reduce the amount of mowing required.
- If this seems too lush a finish, try breaking up the expanse with mown paths at only 2–3cm (1in) high.
- Fit edging bands just below the lawn surface or frame the lawn with a mowing strip of bricks or pavers to eliminate the need for trimming with edging shears.
- Try planting part of the lawn with naturalized bulbs, wildflowers or grassland perennials (see box).
- Move seats, statues, sundials and other ornaments from the lawn, where they interfere with mowing, and re-site them at the sides.
- Thin overhanging tree branches to reduce shade, which can suppress the grass and lead to bare patches that need repair.
- Consider replacing some of the grass with other plants such as moss, clover, wild thyme or one of the creeping mints, which do not need regular mowing.

Dedicated bulb beds need regular maintenance, while bulbs in flower borders risk injury from routine cultivation; planted in grass, though, bulbs will flourish and spread unattended, provided the foliage is not cut down until it withers naturally.

Plants to add to lawns

Relaxing the mowing routine allows plants other than grasses to thrive. Some of these will be 'weeds', of course, although speedwells, daisies, buttercups and clover add a charming speckle of colour and attract various butterflies, moths and bees. In selected areas add clusters of bulbs such as dwarf narcissi, fritillaries and crocuses, wildflowers inserted as plugs – primroses, cowslips, violas, orange or yellow hawkweeds (Hieracium), lady's smock (Cardamine pratensis) and various dwarf campanulas, for example – and even larger hardy perennials such as achillea, asters, geranium species and scabious. Introduce plants that suit the conditions of the site, whether moist, dry, sunny or shaded; control growth rate by never feeding; and cut down all top growth when the last flowers have set and shed seed – leave the cuttings for a week or so and then rake them off for composting.

4

The
PRODUCTIVE
GARDEN

The orthodox approach to cultivating vegetables
and fruit involves an immense amount of digging,
regular hoeing and weeding, and sometimes
intricate pruning or sowing programmes. For these
reasons growing your own is widely dismissed as
adding an impossibly heavy workload to any low-
care garden scheme. But soils can be improved
and maintained without digging, many crops take
up little space and almost look after themselves,
and even fruit growing, which often needlessly
alarms gardeners, can be reduced to a simple and
pleasant routine. So abandon previously held
notions: easy and nutritious edibles can be a
reality, not just a dream.

Although apparently more complicated to tend, vegetables mixed with flowers in borders (page 80) and raised beds (left) are in fact more likely to succeed, hidden from pests and cherished for their incidental beauty.

WHERE TO START

If you are used to kitchen gardening, the areas requiring time and effort will probably be obvious already: crops which need a lot of ground preparation, earthing up, frequent watering or indoor sowing and transplanting, for example. Remember when downsizing that a simpler approach might exist and so avoid your having to abandon a favourite vegetable or fruit altogether. For instance, onions from sets are much easier than from seed, dwarf runner beans in a tub can be attractive and kind to a bad back compared with growing climbing varieties in the ground, and cordon apples on dwarfing rootstocks (see page 94) eliminate the need for major pruning and off-ground maintenance.

Ignore mental images of double digging, barrowloads of manure and tending endless rows of turnips: these date from traditional practices in large kitchen gardens, and today the 'hoe a row' philosophy belongs (if anywhere) on the allotment. While you cannot attain self-sufficiency in the average back garden, despite the temptation to try a

Notable vegetables

The easiest Beetroot, broad beans, carrots, courgettes, curly kale, French beans, loose-leaf lettuce, marrows, perpetual spinach, radishes, ridge cucumbers, salad onions, Swiss chard.

Best yields with little effort Beetroot, carrots, courgettes, dwarf French beans, lettuce, runner beans, tomatoes.

Crops ready within twelve weeks Asparagus peas, beetroot, carrots, Chinese cabbage, claytonia, dwarf beans, early peas, kohl rabi, lettuces, radishes, ridge cucumbers, salad onions, spinach, summer cabbage.

little of everything, you do not require a large area of ground (see page 88) or need to spend a lot of time and effort to achieve worthwhile results.

You need to be hard headed about practicalities, especially when deciding whether or not to grow food in the garden for the first time. Concentrate on crops with good yeilds and that are easy to grow, especially those often unavailable in shops or which taste best when harvested fresh, or simply one or two favourites. List those you particularly like and decide whether it would be sensible or even necessary to grow them. Good produce may be available from farm shops, pick-your-own centres or a veggie-box scheme; crops like cabbages, onions, swedes and maincrop potatoes are more easily produced on a large scale; and a few (cauliflowers and celery, for example) are notoriously difficult to grow well.

Vegetables don't have to be grown in rows or even in a separate plot: the distinction between edible and ornamental plants is artificial; many crops are decorative and blend easily into a flower border, and there are no complicated cultivation rules or demands that mean they have to be grown apart. The basic principles are the same as those for garden flowers: provide good soil management and congenial surroundings, and the plants will do the rest.

Borage (left) is an easy and colourful herb often included in annual flower seed mixtures for attracting wildlife; planted beside a path, parsley (right) is the perfect tidy and productive edging herb, easily accessible for picking.

INTEGRATING CROPS

Kitchen gardens always used to be kept separate and as far from view as possible, an antiquated custom that ignores the fact that plants closest to the house are noticed more and receive the best attention.

Modern gardeners have taken a new look at edible plants and discovered that having crops near to hand is both convenient and visually satisfying, and integrating them with an ornamental scheme is an efficient way of growing them on a smaller, more manageable scale. Chicory, salsify and scorzonera in bloom are as appealing as any conventional border plant, the leaves and flower heads of sea kale are among the most dramatic in the garden; the feathery grace of asparagus and red or gold stems of chard add lively variety and colour; and parsley or carrots make a billowy edging to a flower bed.

You could try lightly forking and composting a small patch in a bed for mingling vegetables with flowers – pelargoniums with dwarf beans and an edging of red loose-leaf lettuce, for example, or dwarf curly kale with

Companion plants

Taken to an extreme, companion planting – growing different plants together to benefit one or more of the partners – can become an esoteric concept based more on anecdote than hard facts, but some combinations undoubtedly work, in the following ways:

nitrogen fixing – clovers, trefoils and lupins are legumes with roots that absorb nitrogen from the atmosphere, which sustains their own growth and sometimes that of nearby plants;

pest control – ground-cover plants hide beetles that prey on slugs, while flowers like phacelia, gaillardia and limnanthes attract pest-predators (see page 109);

protection – some gardeners find that *Tagetes* varieties deter eelworms and white flies, while tomatoes can repel asparagus beetles.

wallflowers for a spring partnership. Perennials like artichokes, cardoons or rhubarb (stunning beside water) team well with flowering perennials; a tripod of runner beans or climbing peas can fit over a group of daffodils to disguise their fading leaves; and tall or scrambling vegetables such as peas, beans, tomatoes and outdoor Japanese cucumbers are easily trained on fences with sweet peas, thunbergia or a perennial climber.

DESIGNING WITH VEGETABLES

This is a logical extension of integrating crops into flower beds. Landscaping with edible plants has been popular since medieval times. Using various crops in ways which exploit their varied colours and forms to create borders or even entire gardens that can be a productive source of food, and a visual delight, is an imaginative way of maximizing the value of limited time and effort.

The classic arrangement is the potager, a formal and very ornate vegetable garden based on a symmetrical pattern of small beds (usually as a divided square, although any pleasing shape is feasible). Plan easy-care paths and edges between beds, and install a permanent centrepiece such as a sundial or a standard gooseberry or rose. Plant vegetables according your own pattern of heights and colours, and add some edible flowers like nasturtiums, evening primroses, violets or sweet Williams for extra colour (don't eat green parts of the flowers, though). Include herbs (pages 90–92) as evergreen ingredients of your scheme and trained fruits (pages 92–4) for their structural, even sculptural contribution.

Among many edible plants that offer colourful highlights are bi-coloured runner beans, striped or mottled French beans, purple peas, blue-leaved leeks, silvery cardoons, golden marjoram, opal basil, purple sage, red cabbages, ruby chard, red Brussels sprouts, red chicory, silver beet,

Vegetables can be grown instead of flowering annuals in spaces between more permanent plants, and can contribute equally appealing colours and textures, such as the gleaming opulence of these red cabbages, in a changing sequence as crops are planted and harvested.

yellow courgettes, red-flowered broad beans and variegated strawberries.

VEGETABLES IN BEDS

Organizing crops on a bed system saves time – because only the specific growing areas need tending rather than a whole plot, and the work is easily divided into manageable units – and labour, because plants are spaced more closely, so their foliage shields the ground from wind and sun. The beds are surface-cultivated from side paths after initial digging and manuring. Beds can be made at ground level or raised to a comfortable working height (see pages 44–7). They may be any length that is convenient, while their width depends on how far you can reach easily from each side without treading on the soil: most gardeners make them about 1.2m (4ft) wide.

If you are restricted to a very limited space or want only a few fresh salads or herbs, smaller beds about 90cm (3ft) each way may be more suitable. These can be further divided with canes to make a number of mini-beds just 30cm (12in) square – an approach known as 'square-foot gardening'. Yields might be modest – nine or ten garlic bulbs, half-a-dozen 'Little Gem' lettuces or a single tomato plant in each square – but they will still be a worthwhile fresh food supplement in exchange for very little space, time and attention. Replant or re-sow each square with a different crop as it is cleared.

A simple salad box

Fill a window box or large wooden container with fresh, moist potting compost, sprinkle seeds very thinly and evenly over the surface, and then cover with a shallow layer of compost: after just a few weeks plants could be tall enough for cutting two or three times with scissors. Sow your own blend of rocket, spinach, coriander, beetroot, oriental greens, lettuce and chicory, or use a bought saladini mixture. For a sequence of leaf salads, start another box every two to three weeks. Similar containers (or a growing bag) can be used for 'mini-vegetables' such as round carrot 'Parmex', lettuce 'Tom Thumb', pea 'Half Pint', radishes and even bushy runner bean 'Hestia'. For extra early or late sowings, cover boxes with glass or plastic film.

PERENNIAL VEGETABLES

Most popular vegetables are annual crops and require sowing or planting at least once every season. You can avoid much of this work by exploring the range of perennial vegetables that give a harvest from the same plants year after year. Yields can steadily increase as plants mature, varieties tend to be more robust and trouble free than annual kinds, and their relative permanence allows beneficial underground processes to evolve – most plants develop partnerships with soil fungi, for example.

Asparagus, rhubarb and globe artichokes are the most familiar (and very ornamental) perennials, but others worth considering include brassicas such as Daubenton's kale, tree collards and perennial ('Nine Star') broccoli; onion relatives like ramsons, garlic chives and everlasting, tree and Welsh onions; and a number of leaf crops for raw or cooked use, such as good King Henry, sea kale, mitsuba, salad burnet, sorrel and salad strains of dandelion. (Chinese and Jerusalem artichokes are true perennials but become weedy and even invasive if not replanted annually.) Add self-seeding annuals or biennials like lamb's lettuce, land cress, rocket, parsley and winter purslane for a diverse mix of self-sustaining vegetables.

CHOOSING VARIETIES

The ever-changing host of vegetable varieties available in seed lists needs careful scrutiny before buying: although they sometimes differ only in minute detail, some are more suitable for allotments, for example, than low-maintenance gardens, and might involve you in extra work. When selecting, check especially:

- size – height and spread will determine how much space or support you need to provide;
- tolerance – frost-hardiness and resistance to ailments or severe weather can save a lot of emergency care;
- performance – make sure they germinate easily and grow predictably;
- adaptability – check they will suit your soil, site, climate and growing method;
- ease of care – self-supporting, self-blanching and easily harvested kinds make life simple.

When you find a variety (not an F1 hybrid) that does well for you, try leaving some of the plants to flower and set seeds, which you can collect, dry and store for sowing the next season. Not only will this save you money, but by identifying plants with special characteristics – those which yield best or survive hard frost or drought – you could gradually isolate a strain that is adapted to your particular garden conditions and therefore easier to grow.

GROWING FERTILITY

In some gardens there is never enough home-made compost (see page 102) to sustain good vegetable crops, many of which are comparatively greedy plants bred to grow fast, yield heavily and then be pulled up, leaving the ground impoverished.

A sound solution to this imbalance is to grow your own fertilizer with a crop of green manure – plants that nourish the soil and the succeeding crops when they are dug in, as well as in a number of other important ways.

- Their rotting foliage and root systems improve soil structure by adding humus.
- They can rest the ground and help it recover from intensive cropping.
- As they grow, their foliage shields the ground from heavy rain, hot sun and drying winds.
- They absorb nutrients and prevent their loss over winter, releasing them again as they rot.
- Their top growth can smother weed seedlings and keep the ground clean.
- They can confuse pests when grown between vegetables and hide pest predators.

Above all, once dug in they can be a free source of fertility, as they decay in the soil and release minerals brought up from deep underground or, in the case of leguminous plants like clover, nitrogen that bacteria in their roots have extracted from the atmosphere.

There are many different green manures to choose from, and your selection will depend on sowing time, how long you can leave it growing and which kind suits your soil. Mustard, phacelia and buckwheat, for example, need only one to three months' growth but do not fix nitrogen and are not hardy; crimson clover enjoys light soil, fixes nitrogen and can be left over winter; lupins are sown up to midsummer on light or acid soils, and fix nitrogen as well as looking attractive in flower.

To reap the benefits of this fertility, single-dig the crop in a few weeks before you want to sow or plant vegetables; for fast, trouble-free decomposition, ideally do this when the ground is warm and before the plants set seed. No-dig gardeners can chop or trample down growth and then plant through this, using it as a green mulch. The top growth of long-term green manures like alfalfa and Essex red clover can be cut several times to soak and produce a liquid feed for other plants (see page 106).

GROWING HERBS

Herbs seem to have all the qualities of the perfect plant – colour, fragrance, diversity, resilience, usefulness and, above all, few demands. Their varied habits and forms suit a range of specific situations in the garden, from majestic back-of-border giants like angelica, boneset or

liquorice to prostrate mats of pennyroyal and Corsican thyme to fill joints between pavers.

Finding enough different kinds to disperse in a flower bed, fill a collection of containers or even stock a whole easily tended herb garden is not difficult provided (as always) you respect their cultural preferences. For example, herbs from Mediterranean regions, like rosemary, sage and most of the artemisias, enjoy a Spartan habitat of dry soil and hot sunshine; woodland species such as chervil, lovage and sweet cicely are happy in shade; and moisture-loving angelica, marsh

Creating and maintaining a herb garden can be demanding compared with muddling up your favourite few herbs with compatible flowers in existing parts of the garden, as here, where French lavender accompanies *Erigeron karvinskianus*.

mallow and meadowsweet revel in damp ground.

Most are self-sufficient and need minimal maintenance.

• There is no need for supplementary feeding, which can dilute flavour and encourage ailments: simply mulch leafy herbs with garden compost, Mediterranean and woody kinds with gravel or grit.

The easiest herbs

For heavy soil: alexanders, angelica, calendula, comfrey, lovage, mint, sorrel, sweet cicely, plus (in sun) borage, chives, fennel and lemon balm

For light soil: anise, arnica, borage, broom, chervil, chives, coriander, foxglove, hyssop, lavender, marjoram, rosemary, tarragon, thyme

For chalky soils: centaury, chicory, cowslip, dianthus, lavender, lemon balm, lily of the valley, lungwort, marjoram, mullein, sage, salad burnet, wormwood

For acid soils: arnica, comfrey, dandelion, foxglove, honeysuckle, pennyroyal, sorrel, sweet cicely

- Regular use takes care of pruning. Picking shoot tips stimulates bushy growth, encourages shapeliness and often prolongs the life of annuals by delaying flowering; perennials are mass-harvested for preserving just before or during flowering time, when flavour is at its peak.
- Some perennials may need replacing every few years if they get leggy or lose their vigour, but you can easily propagate new plants from cuttings or seed, or simply buy new stock. Perennials like bay and rosemary can thrive for decades with regular use or a light annual tidy.
- Although some annuals need deliberate re-sowing each year, many hardy kinds like chervil and parsley will cheerfully self-seed in perpetual colonies.

Widely but mistakenly perceived as utilitarian, fruit trees can be aesthetic or sculptural assets in any garden; here trained and back-lit grape vines fulfil a positively dramatic role.

GARDEN FRUIT

Like herbs, fruit may be a more attractive option for gardeners unwilling or unable to grow a full range of edible crops, and will often give the best return for a surprisingly modest investment of time, care and space. A wide selection of compact soft fruit varieties and tree fruits grafted on dwarfing rootstocks can be grown in a small garden, and occasional light maintenance will result in a sequence of fresh produce (much of it unobtainable or expensive in shops) throughout the year.

Fruit can play an active role in the garden as well as in your diet: like flowering trees and shrubs, fruiting plants add structure and personality to the landscape, but with the bonus of an easily won harvest. When grown in decorative shapes most kinds take up the least space and time, and can be managed with a little easy pruning on a warm summer day (untrained fruit needs more room and comparatively arduous pruning, often during winter). Top or tree fruits like apples and pears may be trained as cordons, fans and other neat shapes on fences, house

walls or beside paths, and can create screens or windbreaks, ornamental fruiting pillars and obelisks in a flower bed, or arches and tunnels over paths. You can sculpt some soft fruits – gooseberries, redcurrants and whitecurrants, for example – as miniature versions of trained fruit trees for a pleasing appearance and enhanced cropping, while raspberries, blackberries and hybrid berries do best on fences and walls fitted with wires for tying in the wandering canes to keep them under control and more productive with less effort. Like children, fruit plants benefit from early basic training and require less restraint later in their lives.

Tree fruit

The most popular of these are apples, plums, cherries, and (in warmer spots) pears, peaches and nectarines. Always buy one of these on an appropriate rootstock for your purpose – apple stocks, for example, vary in vigour from the extremely dwarfing M27, which limits height to about 1.8m (6ft) for cordons and containers, to burly MM111, which supports a height and spread of 6m (20ft), ideal for large orchards and fans on house walls. Other top fruits worth considering include quince, fig and hazelnut (prunings from this make the best pea sticks).

Soft fruit

These are shrubby or rambling plants that make up the middle tier of a plant community. They include popular bush fruits such as gooseberries and black-, red- and whitecurrants, as well as less familiar kinds like jostaberries and goji berries; most can be pruned or trained into decorative and easily harvested shapes. Cane fruits such as raspberries, brambles and hybrid berries (loganberry or tayberry, for example) do not make a permanent branch system and need pruning and tying in to supports, but this annual service is the only major care they need. Large-fruited strawberries need much more attention, and most gardeners find that compact non-running alpine varieties are easier to tend and make productive edging plants for beds and paths.

Practicalities

Fruits are generally easy to please if you indulge their few basic needs. Their flowers will not set fruit in windy or frosty conditions, and a short growing season may prevent a crop ripening fully, so choose positions with maximum sunlight and shelter from cold winds. Gooseberries, though, thrive in cooler conditions, and both rhubarb and redcurrants tolerate shade.

Dig over a metre-square site for each bush or tree, mixing in plenty of compost, and make sure the drainage is good; add a dressing of lime to acid soils when planting stone fruit such as plums, peaches and cherries. Plant firmly at the same depth as the soil mark on stems; support free-standing tree fruits with stakes and tie in trained forms to wires or trellis.

Criteria for choosing fruit

Don't plant fruit on impulse, because an unsuitable type or variety could involve you in a lot of maintenance or corrective work later. Growing any tree is a long-term investment: a healthy apple or pear could easily outlive you, and you can expect at least seven years' productive life from soft fruit (except strawberries, which need renewal every three to four years), so you need to be sure you are making the best and most productive choice for your site.

- Vigour, shape and ultimate size of varieties or rootstocks should match the allocated space to reduce needless pruning.
- Take your soil and climate into account. Plums prefer heavy soil, for example, and most cooking apples do well in mild, wet regions.
- Choose a balanced selection of early, mid-season and late varieties to spread the harvest and avoid waste.
- Early top fruit varieties do not keep well, so grow only enough for immediate use straight from the tree.
- Check any pollination requirements: soft fruits are self-fertile, some tree fruits crop on their own, but many need one or two compatible partners.
- Always buy plants certified in good health and, where possible, tolerant or resistant to pests and diseases.

Neat, productive and easy to prune, cordons of tree fruit like apples and pears make the most of limited space, especially when trained on the slant, as here.

5

LOOKING AFTER the GARDEN

The routine work involved in maintaining the well-being of plants in our care is often a key source of joy to dedicated gardeners but may be an impossible commitment for others. There is always a hard way to carry out tasks like raising plants, controlling weeds or watering during a drought, but happily there exist easier and no less efficient alternatives that might be more appealing to anyone suffering from lack of ability or opportunity. No shame need be attached to looking for a successful short cut if it produces results and releases time to relax and enjoy the garden.

WHERE TO START

Sometimes there seem to be 101 jobs to do in a garden, especially if it is new and still settling down or if bad weather has held things up for a week or two. It may then be hard to appreciate its beauty or adopt a calm, measured approach to the work ahead. But stand a problem on its head and it often becomes a lesson that reveals ways to avoid a similar situation in the future. This is when an inviting garden seat becomes essential.

Pause for a while to reassess why looking after the garden has become a high-maintenance responsibility, and consider some of the ways discussed earlier in which its design or contents might be changed to advantage: this is an evolving process, seldom completed in a single comprehensive makeover. Remember that you can always look for help with any large projects or unappealing chores like mowing or hedge trimming.

Then break down the essential maintenance into realistic stages, perhaps as easy measured projects – it should be possible to target a particular small area or task to complete in a half-hour break from a busy

When starting to reorganize the garden for easier care, look first at structural elements, improving access by laying a simple path (page 96), for example, or enhancing the setting with non-living features like sculpture, ornaments and mirrors (right).

Organizing work

The quickest and least stressful way to cope with a number of apparently pressing demands is to do them one at a time, focusing solely on completing that single task by the most efficient method. Shrewd preparation and precautions, however, can help you simplify and reduce the overall workload. For example:

- **Acquiring plants** (see page 100) – choose appropriate, good-quality plants that suit your site and need the least attention.
- **Watering** (see page 101) – take steps to delay the point when this becomes necessary, and then efficiently water only those plants in need.
- **Feeding** (see page 103) – concentrate on topping up soil fertility every year so that most plants have enough accessible food for the season.
- **Weeding** (see page 105) – identify those weeds that cause the most problems, and prevent these from becoming established.
- **Pruning** (see page 107) – understand the reasons why gardeners prune, so that you can minimize the amount you have to do.
- **Plant health** (see page 108) – explore ways of avoiding, deterring and even deceiving pests and diseases to limit the need to intervene.
- **Wildlife** (see page 109) – re-examine the role of wild creatures in your garden to see where they can help you maintain its well-being.
- **Yourself** (see page 111) – looking after yourself and cultivating a comfortable pace can make the gardening routine a pleasure.

schedule. Make sure the timing suits the plants as well as you: plant a new shrub while it is dormant, for example, and you could avoid a lot of needless follow-on care, whereas later planting, even of container-grown stock, might involve urgent 'rescue' watering in a dry summer.

STARTING WITH PLANTS

The most vulnerable stages in the life of a garden plant (and therefore the most demanding in terms of care and possible risk) are infancy, while it is still developing independence as a seedling, and transplanting, when it is moved from indoors to full exposure outside or from the container in which it was bought to the open ground. A sensible blend of forethought and compromise can help ease plants through these hazardous steps. Always prepare the site thoroughly with plenty of humus before sowing or planting, to avoid the necessity for remedial care later.

Raising your own

Starting plants from seed is simple, satisfying and even compulsive for many gardeners, but once started the process cannot be stopped. Any seed is an embryo plant dried to the point of dormancy and enclosed in a protective coat: supply water and most popular kinds will immediately begin germinating (uncommon plants often need other stimuli as well). At this stage you need to maintain a congenial growing environment – steady moisture levels, an appropriate temperature and adequate ventilation, for example – which requires a lot of commitment if you are sowing indoors.

There are various ways you can avoid some of these extra demands and simplify the process of raising new plants. Hardy varieties, like many vegetables and annual or biennial flowers, are best sown where they are to grow as soon as the ground has warmed up sufficiently in spring. They will tend to look after themselves and often catch up sowings started under glass. If you need earlier results, sow them in a soil-based cold frame or under glass or polythene in a seedbed, and simply keep them covered until they are ready to transplant to the open garden – they will need much less attention growing in the ground than indoors in containers.

Frost-tender kinds such as bedding begonias, petunias or tomatoes need an early start indoors and several weeks' growth in heat and good light. Avoid this intensive care by exploring a garden centre, where there is usually a wide range offered as young plants, hardened off ready to set out in the garden, or as less expensive plugs, which are smaller plants that need growing on in pots or trays until they are sturdy enough to harden off – these have already survived the risky stage of germination and now need less heat and supervision than seeds.

When multiplying your own plants, compare the various methods that work for that particular species or variety.

Hardwood cuttings are easier than soft-tip and semi-ripe cuttings because you can leave them to root unattended in pots outdoors or in the open ground. Allowing a potential new plant to root in its own time while still supported by the parent plant is least demanding of all: layers (low branches rooting where they touch the soil), suckers (young shoots growing straight from the parent's roots) and divisions (portions of the main plant separated with a spade or knife) need only be transplanted to start their independent lives.

Buying plants

When buying a larger plant like a hardy perennial, shrub or tree, check its credentials and condition carefully to avoid unnecessary anxiety or disappointment (see page 58). Buy it when you are ready and at the best time for successful planting – evergreens in early autumn or mid-spring, deciduous varieties while dormant between autumn and spring – rather than as an end-of-sale bargain or untimely impulse.

Give your choice a thorough once-over. In particular you should reject plants that are:

- undernourished – beware limp or yellowing leaves, stunted growth, weedy or mossy surfaces;
- unhealthy – inspect for insect pests and spots, streaks, lesions or blemishes caused by disease;
- neglected – dry compost, forced congested growth, poor or non-existent pruning all make extra work;
- over- or under-grown – freshly potted plugs (loose or easily pulled from the containers) and ageing plants (look for strong roots at the base, dead central portions of perennials or winding roots in the container) are all harder to establish.

WATERING

Two important strategies can economize on the volume and frequency of watering that plants need and the time you devote to this vital task. Plants rely on water to keep them in good physical condition, to supply their roots with dissolved food materials and to top up their internal transport system, which moves nutrients and energy to their extremities.

They take up water from the soil, so the first priority is to provide and prolong an adequate reservoir in the soil. Humus is the ideal storage material – it can absorb many times its own weight of water – and replenishing humus levels is an important annual contribution to delaying the start of watering. You can dig in humus-making material such as garden compost or composted manure, but spreading it as a 5–8cm (2–3in) mulch is more beneficial because this cover also cools the soil surface and prevents water loss by evaporation. Add water-retaining gel crystals to potting compost in containers, and mulch their surfaces.

Pots need routine care, so decide how many you can cope with comfortably and choose varieties wisely. Given sun and good drainage, succulents are forgiving plants, even if watering is occasionally overlooked.

Turning waste into humus

Making garden compost might seem like undertaking an additional chore, but the product can save considerable time and effort by conditioning the soil and improving its water-holding capacity, as well as transforming waste quickly and profitably into free slow-release fertility. Any biodegradable waste can be rotted down in a variety of containers, from a simple netted enclosure to sophisticated bought models with liners, insulation and drip tray to catch the concentrated fluids for liquid feeding. Supplement vegetable waste and weeds with equal quantities of crumpled newspaper or thin card and lawn mowings. If you have only small regular amounts of compostable waste, invest in a wormery instead.

A stalling growth rate, limp or lacklustre leaves, decline in flowering and eventually wilting stems all indicate an exhausted soil reservoir and are urgent cues to start watering. Soak open-ground plants individually, targeting the base of their stems rather than the whole ground surface, and then apply or top up a mulch. In this way you can often space waterings a week or more apart instead of giving everything a little water each evening.

Concentrate first on the neediest subjects, such as seedlings and transplants, leafy vegetables and crops bearing flowers or fruit. Sink pots, tins or sections of drainpipe next to thirsty plants like runner beans and squashes, and direct the water down these to the plants' roots.

Containers may need daily watering in hot dry weather, but you can relieve their thirst by moving them out of strong sunlight or wind. Group them together to maintain a cooler environment and make watering more convenient. In prolonged drought consider plunging smaller pots in large containers of compost or bark, or bury them to their rims in the ground. An automatic trickle system of pipes controlled by a timer attached to a tap can reduce the watering burden.

FEEDING

All plant growth depends on a balanced supply of nutrients that are not only present in the ground but accessible in a form that can be absorbed by active roots – even a potentially fertile soil like clay may not support growth if it is dry or waterlogged, and light sandy soils can be hungry after prolonged rain has dissolved and leached out available plant foods. Wise gardeners pre-empt any shortage by feeding the soil rather than the plants.

When you first make or overhaul a growing area, work in plenty of organic material to provide a reservoir of foods and to sustain the secret life in the soil – microscopic organisms, larger creatures such as worms and beneficial fungi all help release nutrients from humus and turn them into a form available to plant roots. They are not so active (and may die out altogether) in airless compacted or waterlogged ground or in undernourished urban soils and recent building sites: these urgently need a supply of humus worked into the ground, followed by a further dressing applied as a mulch.

This kind of preparation may be sufficient for many plants. A balanced established community whose exhausted top growth is allowed to rot back into the soil every winter can flourish more successfully than an organized border with tidily spaced plants, bare soil and twice-yearly feeding, which often stimulates soft growth susceptible to frost, wind and disorders. If you concentrate on improving the soil, extra feeding often becomes unnecessary.

A handsome, generous pot housing an established and well-grown hosta, the perfect example of how a cherished specimen can make an important statement in the simplified garden.

Areas where supplementary feeding may be beneficial:

- heavily cropped vegetable patches – simply add a further mulch whenever replanting or re-sowing, plus a scattering of slow-release general fertilizer such as blood, fish and bone;
- seasonal containers, where integral feeds in the compost are often exhausted after about six weeks unless specifically identified as slow-release – water every two to three weeks with a low-nitrogen liquid feed;
- larger containers – re-pot or top-dress annually with fresh compost and then mulch; feed vigorous plants after six weeks;
- bedding on light soils after prolonged heavy rain or a wet winter – spread a balanced granular fertilizer around crops;
- ailing plants recovering from any setback, such as drought or nutrient deficiency – water on a liquid foliar feed.

WEEDING

Weeds are all about attitudes. Gardeners generally know what they mean by the expression, and most might agree that nettles, thistles, chickweed and ground elder are undoubtedly weeds, but any personal list of examples would also include less obvious kinds. Primroses, campanulas and honesty can invade beds and paths in a cottage garden, potatoes overlooked after harvest survive as weeds of the next crop, and birds often sow gooseberry, blackberry and strawberry seeds across allotment plots.

Even common weeds, though, are no more threatening than plants in the wrong place, and some have positive value, which may redeem their presence. Many are soil chemists, helping to indicate the soil type (shepherd's cress and scarlet pimpernel like acid ground, for example; stonecrops and hoary plantains indicate lime) and even modifying it: clovers transfer nitrogen from the atmosphere to the soil, where it is available as a fertilizer, and deep-rooted perennial weeds mine the subsoil for valuable minerals that can be salvaged by careful composting. Some such as chickweed and dandelions (after blanching) are edible, and all can be turned into humus and fertility. Identify your particular weeds, and you will usually find that few are pernicious, and even they will wait until you feel inclined to dispatch them.

Excessive tidiness is a human flaw and often the root of anxiety about the garden, but in fact the clean beds to which tidy gardeners aspire invite more weeds, either unearthed as long-dormant seeds or imported by wind and birds, and maintaining a permanently weed-free garden is virtually impossible. A more realistic approach is to start by weeding the ground as thoroughly as possible while it is vacant – before making a new bed, for example, or between plantings. Try to remove perennial weed root fragments, as these almost always regenerate. Then prevent new weeds from invading by mulching wherever practical, using an organic mulch that will also supply humus, or a synthetic membrane that admits rainfall but suppresses weeds. Any weeds that do appear (and these should be few) are easily hoed off or pulled up.

Putting gathered weeds to good use justifies the small amount of work involved in clearing them. Soft, non-seeding annuals belong on the compost heap. Nettles, comfrey, dandelions and plantains are rich sources of minerals if stuffed in a net bag and left to steep in a barrel or tub of water for two or three weeks: use the resulting liquor neat as a general feed. You can safely recycle the nutritious roots of persistent perennials such as bindweed and ground elder by thoroughly drying them on a sunny path before adding them to compost heaps or by rotting them down in a sealed plastic sack.

The easiest kind of pruning involves simple coppicing, by cutting all growth to the ground (raspberries, for example) or just a proportion each year (blackcurrants). These coloured stemmed dogwoods will respond to either routine.

PRUNING

Appreciating why gardeners prune plants and how growth responds can help remove much of the traditional apprehension about the practice, and also reduce the amount you have to do: not all pruning is justifiable in a low-maintenance garden.

Herbaceous plants are pruned annually to clear their dead growth, usually in autumn, although leaving stems until spring helps protect dormant crowns from severe weather and provides habitats for wildlife. Cleared material is all compostable.

Woody plants such as shrubs and trees are pruned to limit size or improve their performance. Cutting back to size is often the result of planting an excessively vigorous variety, which commits you to self-perpetuating maintenance because the harder you prune, the more the plants respond with new growth. Choosing a more restrained kind that is less likely to outgrow its position can help you avoid much of this 'rescue' pruning. Only hedge trimming is a worthwhile example, as you cannot create a dense bushy hedge without cutting back strong-growing plants at regular intervals.

Pruning to improve performance is a more creative or cosmetic procedure that steers and finely tunes a plant's behaviour, rather than constantly trying to curb it. Plants normally find their own balance between new growth and flowers or fruit, but gardeners often want to readjust this to enhance a particular feature: plenty of colourful young stems of dogwoods or bright new foliage on a variegated elder, for example, or more prolific flowering or heavier crops of larger fruits. Each plant has a preferred pruning method, and experts identify a dozen or more different techniques, so always look for the best advice in a good plant encyclopaedia. But remember that, apart from making sure your tools are sharp and every pruning cut clean, the rules are infinitely adaptable.

Pruning tips

There are several rough guidelines that can help to simplify some of the mystique that often makes pruning needlessly obscure or intimidating and therefore seem more onerous than it need be.

- Never cut without a clear reason, for a severed stem cannot be replaced whereas surplus can be removed another day, when you feel like it.
- It is always better not to prune at all than to remove too much or the wrong parts just because a book advises it is pruning time.

- Make pruning every plant a separate project, stand back frequently to assess progress, and stop as soon as you are happy with its appearance.
- Keep things simple: sawing off a whole misplaced branch, for example, is quicker and usually more effective than snipping away anxiously at every twig.
- Cutting out dead, diseased and damaged stems, plus any that overcrowd the centre of a plant, is often all the pruning you need to do.
- Most shrubs are safely pruned to shape immediately after flowering, thus tidying up dead flower heads and generating new flower shoots in a single operation.
- Winter pruning stimulates even more growth, whereas summer pruning encourages more flowers or heavier crops (and is more comfortable to do).

PLANT AILMENTS

It is impossible to avoid pests and diseases in a garden, because they are an essential part of the natural cycle of growth, death and decay. All plant life is finite – 'perennial' is not the same as 'immortal' – and subject to disorders, which are not necessarily the result of any mistake or oversight on your part. You have a lot of choice in the way you anticipate and respond to their appearance, but the most realistic low-maintenance approach is always to avoid trouble before it arrives.

Diseases

These are caused by living organisms such as bacteria, fungi or viruses, which are transmitted from one plant to another, but disease-like symptoms are also caused by physical disorders resulting from environmental threats such as bad weather, starvation and over-feeding, drought or waterlogged soil. They often (but not exclusively) afflict plants that are weak, stressed or growing in the wrong place.

Prevention is usually easier and more effective than treatment. Start with healthy plants that suit the soil and position, choose resistant or tolerant varieties wherever possible, plant them in thoroughly prepared sites, grow them well, inspect them regularly for early symptoms, and react promptly and firmly if trouble strikes.

First diagnose a problem accurately to see if it is merely seasonal (frost damage, for example), cosmetic (the fused or distorted growth called fasciation) or cultural (iron deficiency). Cutting off affected foliage or branches can limit the spread of a disease such as fireblight. If simple remedies are insufficient, your choice then lies between isolation and chemical treatment, which is often unpredictable and rarely saves a badly affected victim, or simply culling and destroying the plant to prevent recurrence and further spread.

Pests

Nature is full of food chains, with every organism feeding on another below it and in turn becoming the prey of the next one above. Plants are the bottom link in a chain, and every garden plant supplies food for particular insects or larger creatures. Whether you regard these as pests depends on your attitude: the caterpillars of some beautiful butterflies are often acceptable, for example, but not those of cabbage whites when they infest vegetables.

As with diseases, total elimination is a forlorn ideal, and it is more reasonable to tolerate a low level of incidence, while appreciating that only a small minority of pests ever cause serious or widespread problems. These can often be avoided by growing a diverse community of plants so that individual targets are dispersed and hidden among unrelated neighbours. Varieties resistant to specific pests such as eelworms or root aphids are available; various barriers, traps and deterrents can intercept or confuse slugs, moths and other flying insects.

Simple remedies are often the best. Caterpillars, snails, weevils and harmful beetles can be picked off and despatched by hand, while a forceful jet of water will knock aphids and other small pests from plants. Biological controls are available for some specific pests – vine weevils and greenhouse whiteflies, for example. Some manual and non-chemical treatments are time and labour intensive, however, and you may prefer to use a pesticide. Wherever possible, resort to these only in emergencies, because most are indiscriminate and kill many beneficial creatures. Always choose one that is specific and of short-lived potency, and apply it only to affected plants, strictly according to the directions.

Enlisting wildlife

Food chains extend beyond plants and the creatures that feed on them, to include higher links that prey on the pests themselves. Simply encouraging insectivorous birds and predators like hoverflies or lacewings can help achieve a situation where pest and predator are in equilibrium. Feed garden birds and supply them with nest boxes; provide beneficial insects with winter accommodation and flat-topped or nectar-rich flowers on which to browse; and construct a pond to host frogs and toads, which feed voraciously on slugs. An unobtrusive heap of autumn leaves might protect a hedgehog (another predator of slugs and snails) over winter; a neat pile of branches and prunings can shelter smaller allies like ground beetles and millipedes. Remember that chemical treatments can also harm friendly creatures.

Possibly the most important feature in any garden is the seat where you start the process of planning and organizing a less demanding care routine, and end by enjoying the time and commitment you have saved.

LOOKING AFTER YOURSELF

Remember that you always have the final choice about how much gardening you undertake and when you do it.

Only take on as much as you can manage, work when the weather is congenial and you feel motivated, and stop before you are tired. Assemble all the tools and materials you need before starting any task, adopt a gentle relaxed approach, and congratulate yourself at the end of it. Focus on what you have achieved, rather than on what remains to be done – that's for another time.

Even if opportunities are few, make a point of sitting in the garden whenever you can, just while you have a cup of tea, perhaps, or a glass of wine. Gardens are to live in as well as look after, and sitting outside in the one you tend is not a waste of time but a relaxing, inspiring and even healing moment in the day when you can enjoy and appreciate the results of your lighter, more manageable gardening efforts.

INDEX

Page numbers in *italics* refer to captions to the illustrations

Hearing is a **tiger's** sharpest sense—it's five times stronger than a human's.

Green algae can grow in **polar bears'** fur if they stay too hot for too long.

Flamingos' diet of shrimp and algae gives them their distinctive color. They can also drink upside down!

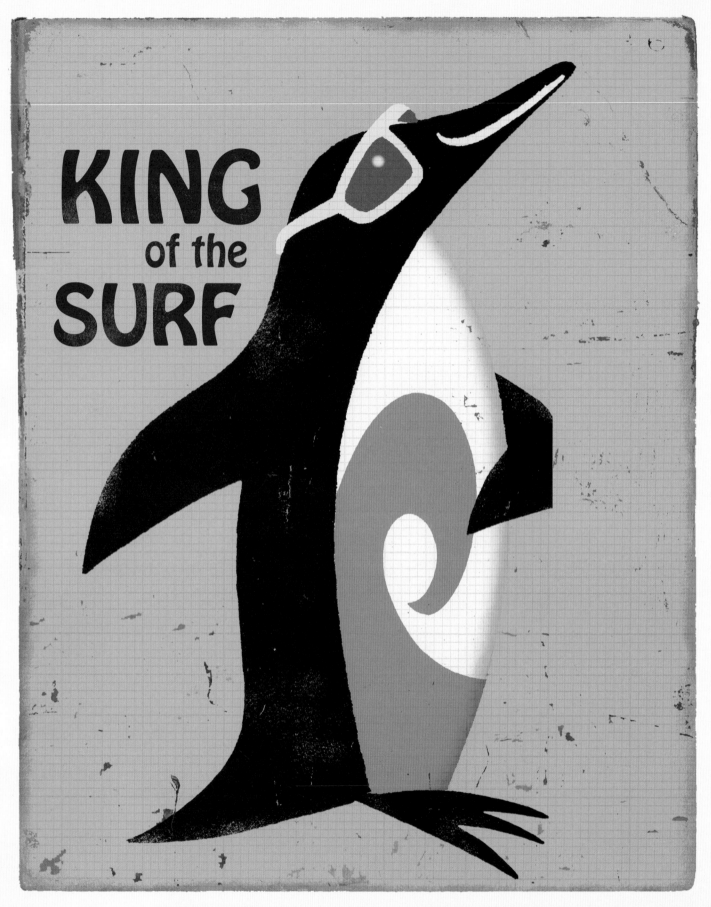

King penguins love to catch a wave and surf onto shore.

Sunlight gives **goldfish** their orange pigment.

Iguanas move into the shade to lower their body temperature.

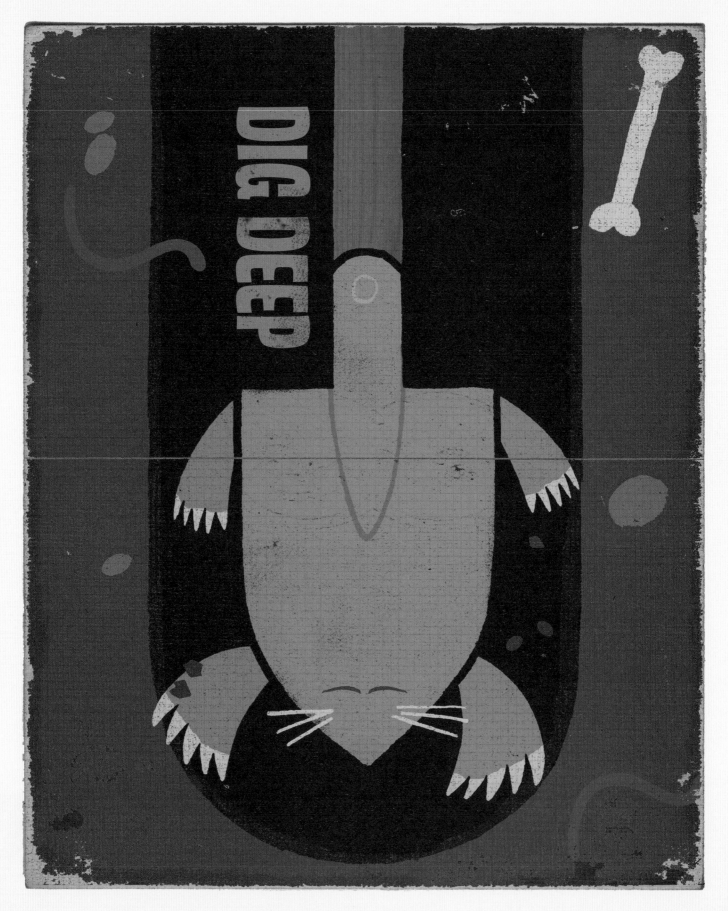

Moles can tunnel 300 feet and eat half their body weight in one night.

Bears sleep through the winter (without pooping!) for up to six months.

Every **dog** has a unique nose print.

Sharks are always growing new teeth to replace those that fall out.

Kangaroos balance on their tails to kick with both feet.

Monkeys split open bananas from the bottom up—it's easier that way!

Hormones make some male **monkeys** go bald.

Keeping their skin moist by showering is important for **elephants'** health.

Rats spend a third of their lives washing themselves.

Bees talk to one another by dancing in patterns.

Pigeons have been decorated by the army for delivering messages during wars.

Giraffes use their 21-inch-long tongues to clean themselves all over—including their ears.

FEED it and WEEP

Chewing makes **crocodiles'** tear ducts spill watery droplets.

Dolphins sleep with one eye open, while resting one half of their brain at a time.

Lions hunt at night, thanks to their ability to see well in the dark.

and **MRS.**

Earthworms are both male and female at the same time.

See the LIGHT

Electric eels can produce enough electricity to power ten lightbulbs.

Turn a **blind** eye

Rabbits are very nearsighted.

Tigers have binocular vision—their eyesight is about six times stronger than humans' at night.

Humans' intelligence means we can do things that other animals cannot—like read this book!

For Van, Becca, Gabriel, Lottie, and Imogen

First U.S. edition 2013

Library of Congress Catalog Card Number 2012943660
ISBN 978-0-7636-6563-0

12 13 14 15 16 17 TLF 10 9 8 7 6 5 4 3 2 1

Printed in Dongguan, Guangdong, China

This book was typeset in Delargo DT Infant.
The illustrations were created digitally.

TEMPLAR BOOKS

an imprint of Candlewick Press
99 Dover Street
Somerville, Massachusetts 02144
www.candlewick.com